A GIRL GOES INTO THE WOODS

A GIRL GOES INTO THE WOODS

Selected Poems

Lyn Lifshin

The New York Quarterly Foundation, Inc.
New York, New York

NYQ Books™ is an imprint of The New York Quarterly Foundation, Inc.

The New York Quarterly Foundation, Inc.
P. O. Box 2015
Old Chelsea Station
New York, NY 10113

www.nyqbooks.org

First Edition

Set in New Baskerville

Layout and Design by Raymond P. Hammond
Cover Photograph, "Sleep Anywhere," © 2010 Eleanor Leonne Bennett
http://eleanorleonnebennett.zenfolio.com/

Author Photograph by Albert Jordan

Library of Congress Control Number: 2013932938

ISBN: 978-1-935520-32-0

A GIRL GOES INTO THE WOODS

Contents

I DON'T KNOW WHAT YOUR EYES HAVE DONE TO ME

GOING HOME

THE DEEPER YOU GO

LOOKING FOR THE LOST VOICES

IN THE DARKNESS OF NIGHT

GALE OF THE SUN, THE ANGELS DON'T FLY

PLEASE NUZZLE SHEETS I'VE LEFT MY SCENT IN

ISN'T IT ENOUGH HOW IT SLAMS BACK?

HAVEN'T YOU EVER LUSTED FOR THOSE RED SHOES?

HOW CAN YOU EXPECT ME NOT TO WRITE ABOUT DEATH?

AFTER A DAY OF COLD RAIN

COMFORT AND LONGING

THE BELLY DANCING SKIRT

BLACK VELVET GIRL

(autobiography)

BUT INSTEAD HAS GONE INTO WOODS

A girl goes into the woods
and for what reason
disappears behind branches
and is never heard from again.
We don't really know why,
she could have gone shopping
or had lunch with her mother
but instead has gone into
woods, alone, without the lover,
and not for leaves or flowers.
It was a clear bright day
very much like today.
It was today. Now you might
imagine I'm that girl,
it seems there are reasons. But
first consider: I don't live
very near those trees and my
head is already wild with branches

I WAS FOUR, IN DOTTED

Swiss summer pajamas,
my face a blotch of
measles in the small
dark room over blue
grapes and rhubarb,
hot stucco cracking.
17 North Seminary.
That July Friday
noon my mother was
rushed in the gray
blimp of a Chevy
north to where my
sister Joy would be
born two months
early. I wasn't
ready either and
missed my mother's
cool hands, her
bringing me frosty
glasses of pineapple
juice and cherries
with a glass straw
as Nanny lost her
false teeth, flushed
them down the toilet
then held me so tight
I could smell lavender
and garlic in her
braided hair, held
me as so few ever
have since, as if
not to lose more

SOME AFTERNOONS WHEN NOBODY WAS FIGHTING

my mother took out
walnuts and chocolate
chips. My sister and
I plunged our fingers
in flour and butter
smoother than clay.
Pale dough oozing
between our fingers
while the house filled
with blond bars rising.
Mother in her pink dress
with black ballerinas
circling its bottom
turned on the Victrola,
tucked her dress up into
pink nylon bloomer pants,
kicked her legs up in the
air and my sister and I
pranced thru the living
room, a bracelet around
her. She was our Pied
Piper and we were
the children of Hamlin,
circling her as close as the
dancers on her hem

NIGHTS IT WAS TOO HOT TO STAY IN THE APARTMENT

We drove to the lake, then stopped
at my grandmother's. The grown-ups
sat in the screened porch on wicker
or the glider whispering above the
clink of ice in wet glass. Spirea and
yellow roses circled the earth under
stars. A silver apple moon. Bored
and still sweaty, my sister and I
wanted to sleep out on the lawn
and dragged out our uncle's army
blankets and chairs for a tent. We
wanted the stars on our skin, the
small green apples to hang over
the blanket to protect us from bats.
From the straw mats, peonies glowed
like planets and if there was a breeze,
it was roses and sweat. I wanted
our white cats under the olive green
with us, their tongues snapping up
moths and whatever buzzed thru the
clover. For an hour the porch
seemed miles away until itchy with
bug bites and feeling our shirts fill
with night air, my hair grows curlier,
our mother came to fold up the blankets
and chairs and I wished I was old
enough to stay alone until dawn or
small enough to be scooped up, asleep
in arms that would carry me up the
still-hot apartment stairs and into
sheets I wouldn't know were still
warm until morning

SITTING IN THE BROWN CHAIR WITH
LET'S PRETEND ON THE RADIO

I don't think how the
M&M's that soothe
only made my fat legs
worse. I'm not thinking
how my mother will
die, of fires that could
gulp a mother up, leave
me like Bambi. I'm not
going over the babysitter's
stories of what they did to
young girls in tunnels, of
the ovens and gas or have
nightmares I'll wake up
screaming for one whole
year wanting someone to
lie near me, hold me as if
from then on no one can get
close enough. I don't hear
my mother and father yelling,
my mother howling that if
he loved us he'd want to buy
a house, not stay in the apart-
ment he doesn't even pay
her father rent for but get
a place we wouldn't be
ashamed to bring friends.
What I can drift and dream
in is more real. I don't want
to leave the world of golden
apples and silver geese. To
make sure, I close my eyes,
make a wish on the first hay
load of summer then wait
until it disappears

BEING JEWISH IN A SMALL TOWN

someone writes kike on
the blackboard and the
Ks pull thru the
chalk, stick in my

plump, pale thighs.
Even after the high
school burns down the
word is written in

the ashes. My under-
pants' elastic snaps
on Main St. because
I can't go to

Pilgrim Fellowship.
I'm the one Jewish girl
in town but the 4
Cohen brothers

want blond hair
blowing from their
car. They don't know
my black braids

smell of almond.
I wear my clothes
loose so no one
dreams who I am,

will never know
Hebrew, keep a
Christmas tree in
my drawer. In

the dark, my fingers
could be the menorah
that pulls you toward
honey in the snow

GOING TO THE CATHOLIC SCHOOL

once a year, bundled in wool
peacoats and snow pants,
mufflers dotted with ice crystals
tightly around our faces so the
incense we were sure would be
too thick to breathe in wouldn't
make us sneeze. Under our
snow pants, soft corduroy jeans
and our thickest gloves, covered
mittens: we had heard about
rulers smashing bones and skin,
that patent leather shoes were
forbidden. Something about the
stained glass light on the pale
nuns with enormous crosses
and rosaries kept us huddled and
close, walking with only side-
long glances at the Jesus with
bleeding chest, as scary as *The
Thing* where Jessica, whose
father was a minister, shrieked
when the blob filled the screen.
We didn't know why the Catholic
girls couldn't come to our school
but would come later, in high
school. Or why everything
had a smell we never smelled
anywhere else, wondered how
we'd ever catch up in Latin when
we had to. The dark-haired girls
with their dangling faces of

Mary they kissed before a ball
game and tests seemed as exotic
as what was hidden under their
white confirmation dresses,
flesh later we heard would writhe
and twist and do the wild thing
since it would be OK once
they confessed

YELLOW ROSES

pinned on stiff tulle,
glowed in the painted
high school moonlight.
Mario Lanza's *Be My
Love*. When Doug
dipped I smelled
Clearasil. Hours in
the tub dreaming of
Dick Wood's fingers
cutting in, sweeping
me close. I wouldn't
care if the stuck
pin on the roses
went thru me,
the yellow musk
would be a wreathe
on the grave of that
awful dance where
Louise and I sat
pretending we didn't
care, our socks fat
with bells and fuzzy
ribbons, silly as we
felt. I wanted to be
home, wanted the
locked bathroom to
cry in, knew some
part of me would
never stop waiting
to be asked to dance

DREAM OF THE PINK AND BLACK LACE, JUST LIKE THE EVENING GOWN

my favorite in high school,
a dress I'd wanted to see
marked down and finally wrote
the store, even then, able
to get what I wanted

more easily on paper. I
told them how often I'd come
back, hoping it would be marked
down and dashed up with my
mother when they agreed
to lower the price.

I feel the swirl of those
gowns I ran my hand through,
terrified mine wouldn't
be there, then carrying it as
carefully as a baby of blown glass.

It was so full my waist
looked tiny inside it
with hoops and an eyelet bustier.
The dress took up half
my mother's closet,

less space than I did in her,
especially after she had me.
I don't think I wore it again, too
dressy, too much lace to pack.
But I can see it near the yellow

and the pink and white gauzy gowns,
swirling strapless, a part of 38
Main Street I expected to always
be as it was, like my mother
waiting for me to fill it

HAIR

In Brooklyn one
love's aunt plotted,
made an appointment
to have it done,
cut in a flip

a present for me
like the scratchy
nylon gowns I
never wore when I
left to marry

An uncle said before
he died he wished
he could see it
short. After

the wedding I
pulled pins out of
that stiff hive
for a week, afraid
to touch it

When I taught in
high school I had
to wear it up,
sprayed it one
gray morning
with flit as

if it was a
living, flying
thing that
shouldn't, like
my life seemed
that October,

unreal, I was
afraid to touch
it, all his family
tried to pull it
back into velvet,

twist it, pin
it choke, they said
they wanted to see
my eyes but I
know they suspected
me of being a
hippie, a witch.

The college that
said I couldn't stay
on white cold paper
wrote first *can't you look*
more professional

and dignified. Wear
it up. The brother-
in-law would pull
it, sneer, ask if I'd
seen the mad

hair girl in
The Munsters. I
heard that the whole TV season.
Later I learned that

what grew out of
the dark where I
couldn't reach
like dreams or
poems was beautiful,

shouldn't be
squeezed into,
changed into
something different.

But those years,
apologizing, stuffing
that sun-bleached red
under my collar

straightening it in
what was OK for the
early seventies and
never letting it

go where it wanted

milkweed, wild
flowers, poems,
animals, a dream

hair like someone
who couldn't, hadn't
wouldn't admit, didn't
know it had a
life of its own

FAT

Some of it I've
given away, I guess that
comes from thinking
nobody could
want it.
Fat. Something you
take in and just
can't use.
It hangs around
reminding you of what
wasn't totally
digested, a layer of heavy
water, grease

having so
much I'd dream the
4:30 tall thin
shadow thighs were
me, pressing so hard it
hurt, a
punishment squeezing
myself into
me, into
what I didn't
want. Afternoons
with the shades drawn
examining and hating what
I saw, longing for one of those
svelte bodies

I put the
scales back, would have
beat myself with
rubber chains

when I was 12 I bought a
rubber girdle, nobody
knew I peeled it off with the
door locked

Somebody once said
you'll never get
cold this winter
fat legs
like that

How could something like fat ever
protect you from anything
outside being only an
extension of yourself, cells
spreading, making you
more vulnerable,
fat people having more
places to bruise
or scar

I sat in a room and
watched the
river when
other girls
were going across the
state line,
were necking in cars at
Lake Bomoseen
despising those
layers I
didn't need

belly that
I hated and squeezed into
clothes a size
too small, hips, but
worse, thighs, I
hated them
most, spreading out
on benches
for basketball practice

Once I lay on my
back cycling air until
the room spun

white waves of the body,
I was so ashamed I wouldn't go
to the beach

My mother always
said *Yes, you're pretty,*
eat and I curled
into myself
eating what made
me worse

tho I wanted to
wear pleats
and be delicate

In one store a
man asked her
Is it difficult
having one daughter

who's so lovely? and I
hated my sister for being
blond, her body

like a Keane
waif, I was jealous of
her eggnogs and
chocolate,
how meat had to be
coaxed to her
bones

You can't camouflage,
hold anything in
that long. It explodes,
a rubber girdle pops,
elastic
letting go.
Then they know
that there's more
than you can
handle

Look at me now and
you say *but those
thin wrists*

Listen, when I weigh
over a hundred I
break out in
hives. We

all think of the way
we were

especially when it
comes to what we
don't love

Once when I was
walking home from
school the elastic
on my underpants died.
The next day someone
wrote kike on the
blackboard.
Both I knew were a result
of fat

I've never been good
at getting rid of
what I can't use
but that's when I
knew that I had to

that round face with
glasses, bulging
thighs. You know

when some man says
love it's still
hard to believe

If I wear my clothes too short, it's to
remind myself (I still
avoid mirrors,
glass) that my

legs are not
unlovable, I

want you to see I finally am
someone you might
want to dance with

this me waiting under-
neath on the
side lines

years of
getting down to

But it really is
sweetest close
to the bone

LIPS

Yours, honey, were so perfect,
a little rosebud mouth, not
those puffed-up blubbery
things, my mother says when
I pointed out the models'
collagen petals. "Roses," my
mother always says, "that's
what yours were, a nice
tiny nose. That's from your
father. One good thing. Not
a big ugly one like I've got."
I think of my mother's lips,
moving close to my hair, how
her breath was always sweet.
"Too-thin lips, like your father's,
show stinginess." She was
right. A man who couldn't give
presents or love, a good word
or money. I only remember
three things he told me and
all begin with **Don't** tho my
mother said stories came from
those lips, that he brought me a
big dog. I only remember the
thinness of his lips, how his
death meant I wouldn't have to
leave school to testify for the
divorce. Lips. When I came home
from camp I found *Love Without
Fear* in the bathroom and read
"if a girl lets a man put his tongue
on her lips down there, she'll let
him do anything," and then some-
thing about deflowering. A

42

strange word I thought trying to
imagine flowers down there, rosebuds
not only on my mouth, a petal
opening, but a whole bush of petals,
a raft of roses someone kneeling
would take me away on, a sea of
roses, flowers and my lips the
island we'd escape to

MORE HAIR

In college I wore
it up, was accused of
someone taking my
test for me

relatives were always
smoothing it down, putting
pins in it, as if it
was some strange night
beast, animal, dark
weeds to cut back

When I was six in the
cottage I combed it
straight in the wet
sun but it didn't
stay, it was like

fat, like my fat
thighs that looked
thin in the late
afternoon shadows

they had their fat
way in the mirror
in the damp room
though I wanted to be
skinny with long,
straight hair,

dieted until
I passed out, put
Curl Free on it and
just got it orange,
as plastic as a broom.

In those years, people
used to laugh, sneer
hippie. I tucked it up
into itself for in-laws,
bosses, English
examining committees,
and superintendents,
knotted it tight
as a hair ball
inside a cat, a
pearl waiting,
nests for some
thing inside. I

hated not being able
to let it down, hated
twisting it, twisting
myself into what was
neat, small, expected

I was sorry I wasn't
Indian, wished that
it would grow long
enough to hold out
buildings, as if I
could climb out into
my new self that way

WRITING CLASS, SYRACUSE WINTER

write, he said looking
like an even craggier
Lincoln, *your impressions*
the next 4 days, details
of a walk across campus.
Even now I remember I
wore a strawberry wool
skirt, matching sweater.
There was bittersweet
near the Hall of Language.
I curled in a window
ledge of a cave in Crouse,
an organ drifting thru
smooth, warm wood. I
could let the wine-
dark light hold me, slid
on the ice behind where a
man with a blue mole
picked me up, my notes
scattering up Comstock.
Torn tights, knees snow
kissed the skin off. I was
hypnotized by that
huge growth, said yes
tho I only half remembered.
Upstairs icicles clotted,
wrapped glass in gauze.
There must have been some
one who didn't call. Blue
walls, ugly green bedspread,
Dorothy popping gum, eating
half a tuna sandwich before
we'd lie in bed with the
lights out wondering what

it would be like to have
Dr. Fox with his red beard
go down on us as we
braided and rubbed our
mahogany hair dry and I
tried to figure out what to
do with the bittersweet,
torn knees, ragged maples,
didn't believe I'd ever
have anything to write about

YOU UNDERSTAND THE REQUIREMENTS

we are
sorry to have to
regret to
tell you
sorry sorry
regret sorry that you have
failed

your hair should have been
piled up higher

you have failed to
pass failed
your sorry
regret your
final hair comprehensive
exam satisfactorily
you understand the requirements

you understand we are
sorry final

and didn't look as professional
as desirable
or sorry dignified
and have little enough
sympathy for 16th century
sorry English Anglicanism

we don't know doctoral
competency what to think and
regret you will sorry not
be able to stay
or finish

final regret your disappointment
the unsuccessfully completed best
wishes for the future
it has been a
regret sorry the requirements
the university policy

please don't call us

ORALS

Half of them
cough, the one
with the limp wittily
grunts towards me
you remind me of
Theda Bara, a distant
relative I blush be-
cause it's true.
Already
his eyes are
full of no.
Smoke boils up from the
table, the scraped faces
freeze on me until I
wish I hadn't come

Suddenly this glass voice
clangs *And what do you*
think of adultery? Now
it is not easy to be
clever under his
fluorescent glare but
I look right back and
ask how that's
relevant. He doesn't
like that at all

scratches an ear and wants
to know if Tottel's 3rd
cousin by a later
marriage of course
is significant in 19th

century bibliography and
my God he is serious I
sweat inside my specially
lengthened drab gray suit

beginning to think of
oceans, imagining that
walls could drift
out slowly, even
the floor slide away.
Not able to suppose
just then why Marvell
didn't write the
same poems that Donne
did briefly in 72
seconds, or where
Fulke Greville was
while Spenser was
having his fire

The two faces I thought
I knew keep dissolving.
Their eyes float to
shelves where words
live predictably

Are you certain of
those dates a British
accent whines thru
teeth that have never
lived outside New
York City. A stranger
bends into his shoes

as if the laces were
nastily disappointing

We know your record
the Milton man spits
thru a belch but you
understand the require-
ments, couldn't you
just have a baby?

THE NO MORE APOLOGIZING THE NO MORE LITTLE LAUGHING BLUES

apologizing for going to
school instead of having
a job that made money
or babies
pretending I took the bus
to an office, paper
clips in my ears
and never that I was
reading Wyatt,
writing my own dreams
in the dust under the

Apologizing for my
hair, wild gypsy
hair that fell out of
every clip, the way the
life I started dreaming
of did. Apologizing for
the cats

You know if someone said my skirt
was too short, I explained
or said sorry but never that
I finally loved my legs

I spent years apologizing for not
having babies, laughing
when someone pulled
a baby Gerber jar out
of the closet and held it in
front of my eyes like
it was a cross. Or a star

I should have thrown that
thru the glass. I didn't

53

need to explain the music
I liked. One friend said *that's
noise.* Another said *isn't denim for
children?* I laughed the apologizing
"oh I don't want no trouble" laugh
over the years, pretending to cook,
pretending to like babying
my husband

The only place I said what I meant
was in poems. That green was like some
huge forbidden flower until it grew so
big it couldn't even fit in the house,
pulled me out a window
with it toward Colorado

I apologized for being what
they thought a woman was by being
flattered when someone said
you write like a man and for not being what they thought
a woman, for the cats and leaves
instead of booties, for the poems

When someone said *how much
do you get paid,* I pretended,
pretended, pretended. I could not
stop trying to please:

The A, the star, the good girl
practically stamped on my forehead.
The spanking-clean haunted half my life.
But the poems had their own life

and mine finally followed
where the poems were growing,

warm paper skin growing
finally in my real bed
until the room stopped spinning for
good the way it used to when I dressed
up in suits and hairspray

pretending to be all those things I
wasn't: teacher, good girl, lady,
wife. I was writing about lovers
for years before I'd felt,
when I was still making love just on
the sheets of paper

When the poems first came
out one woman I drove to school with
said *I can't take this.* Another said
*I don't know, this can't be the you
I know, so brutal, violent.
Which is the real?*

The man I was with moved to
the other side of the bed.
This was worse than not having
babies. His mother said they
always knew I was odd

my clothes, my hair,
the books I brought to bed.
They said I never seemed like
one of them

My own family thought it was
OK but couldn't I write of things that
were pleasant? They wanted to know how much
I got paid and why I didn't write for
The Atlantic

Look, I still have trouble saying
no. I want most of you to
care about what I'm thinking,
maybe even to
want my hair

It's true, I put a No Smoking sign up
on the door but twice I have
gotten out ashtrays

But I have stopped being grateful to
be asked to read
or to always have
a lover right there beside me

It's still not easy to get off the
phone, tell a young, stoned poet
it's a bore to lie with the
phone in my ear like a
cold rock while he goes on
about the evils of money,
charging it to my phone

But now when I hear myself laughing
that apologizing laugh, I know what
swallowing those black seeds can
do and I spit them out. Like tobacco
(something men could always
do). Look, nothing good grows from the
I'm sorry, sorry, only those dark
branches that will get you from inside

THE PEARLS

An engagement present from my husband's parents,
shoved in a drawer like small eggs waiting to hatch,
forgotten. They seemed like something in a high school
photograph. I'd have preferred a large, wrought iron pendant,
beads that caught the sun. Pearls were for *them*

and I was always only a visitor, tho he said he wished
I'd call him Dad. Sam was all I could get out.
It was hard to throw my arms around him, to bubble
and kiss. And not just because they thought
me a hippie, a witch, thought I took

their son's car and stamps and coin collections.
Pearls wouldn't go with my corduroy smocks, long, black,
ironed hair. They didn't blend with my hoops of onyx
and abalone that made holes in my ears but caught the light.
Pearls might have gone with the suits I threw away,
no longer a graduate student trying to please.
They weren't suitable for days with a poet hidden in trees
or for throwing up wine in toilet bowls after poetry readings
where I shook and swore not to let anyone see. My spider medallion
is in at least eight poems. Pearls remind me of the way I thought

I was: studious but not wild, not interesting. But I put those pearls
on last night tho I hadn't planned to wear them. They didn't seem ugly
or apt to choke, seemed gentle and mild as so little is in my life
these days. I slept in nothing but those pearls, they seemed part of me

I WEAR MY HAIR LONG

to remember old boyfriends'
aunts making appointments,
telling stylists to cut it short,
in a flip. I wear my hair long
to protest against all the
shaved heads at Auschwitz,
against the threats of PhD
examiners to look more
professional and dignified.
I want it to smell of lilac wind,
want my old cat in its warmth.
I long to hang my hair out
windows to shy lovers, a
dare, a disguise to throw you
off. I envy Indian women
who can sit on the black river
pouring down their backs.
My hair begs to be touched,
caught in your fingers,
your teeth. It smells of lilies,
gardenias, some animal you
never want not near once
you've stroked it. Taste
it and you'll want to wear
it, wrap dreams deep in it
when leaves start to change.
Pale as a flag made of the
moon it will guide you, lead
you in deeper

ALL NIGHT THE NIGHT HAS BEEN

lightening with moths

white behind the walnuts

If a woman couldn't sleep
and came to this window
in this light her skin
would glow like bones

Clouds over the full moon
even with the wind

What would have been
nuts looks like limes
on the white stones,

it sounds like some-
one tapping on a glass
coffin. It sounds

like someone tapping
from within the tree

SOME NIGHTS I'M RAISEL DEVORA DREAMING OF OLD HOUSES IN RUSSIA

of licorice hair fire
licks as lace is
scorched, turns ash
before the wedding
and the bride's bones
are dust in the
rose light green
is sucked from as sun
sets in the afternoon.
Some unknown
aunt I could have
been named for maybe,
wild, intense as rare
tea roses or Rashmi
Rose incense burned in
a room the walls
pulled from floats
through frames that
are like mirrors, her
raw cheeks like
cherries in the rain
or blood from a wild
deer running, turning
snow color of plums

THE DAUGHTER I DON'T HAVE

jolts up in the
middle of the night
to curl closer than
skin, pink-tongued
in a flannel dress
I wore once in some
story. I part her
hair, braid her
to me as if to
keep what I can't
close, like hair
wreathes under
glass in New
England. Or maybe
pull the hair into
a twist above the
nape of her neck,
kiss what's exposed
so wildly part of
her stays with me

DREAM OF IVY

you know the story of
the woman in a
turret and how ivy
puts its fingers
across the moon.
And besides, no one
could hear. Ivy
that grows like
kudzu in the
deepest part of Georgia
swallowing up a
single house
in one night. I would
have lowered my long
hair to a lover,
lured him with blood
in a bottle, each
drop a ruby with
a poem etched on it.
Or carved my initials
in the gray stone
around his heart. I'd
have talked to the
birds or waited,
slept 20 years, given
away my children.
Only I was outside
trying to get in

I DON'T KNOW WHAT YOUR EYES HAVE DONE TO ME

(relationships)

DRIFTING

things I have and
don't have
come from this
moving between
people like
smoke. I've been
waiting the way
milkweed I
brought inside two
years ago stays
suspended, hair in the
wind it seems to
float, even its
black seeds don't
pull it down
tho you don't under-
stand how any-
thing could stay
that way
so long

WHY AEROGRAMS ARE ALWAYS BLUE

Because of the distance to you.
Because the wind fades,
dries out the verbs
until the background they've
leaned against blends
with the sky.
The blue reflects your eyes.
No, that's a lie, I don't
remember them, only the
feeling in my hands, some
thing longing, aching the
blue in my veins a fast
blue burning barriers

NOT QUITE SPRING

Baby, you know I get high
on you, come back with me
whispering in her ear.
It was all she could do to say
no, spring leaves budding,
his hand on her breast,
crocus smell and
everything unfolding.
She gasping *I want, I*
would but instead hurrying
back to the windowless room
where she locks the heavy door.
Lemons are rotting on her pillow,
she studies her nipples,
nyloned crotch in mirror
then hugs her huge body to sleep

CAT CALLAHAN

being fat until
that spring, I still
felt fat on Main Street
in my town but

not when the science
fair went north,
Burlington for 3 days,
I met the kind of

long-haired boy I
hadn't. The photograph
with my eyes huge,
how the cop downstairs

groaned when he screamed
in with that Ford.
Relatives squirmed at
his name. By June I

unbuttoned my sweater,
wriggling in a back-
seat near Champlain
Al Martino's *Oh My Love*

I've hungered for so,
the pink check dress
wrinkling a long time
as things inside
unchained were saying
yes, yes tho I didn't

FITZI IN THE YEARBOOK

grin muffled but
sneaky, slithering
out like his penis
did in the drive-in
a June before I could
imagine anything so
slippery sliding up,
let alone inside
me after months of
Saturdays in my
mother's gray apartment,
my sister giggling
behind the couch,
a tongue pressing
between lips should
have been a warning in
the blue Chevy I felt
he was all whale
crashing with his
now you've done
this to me, you have
to, everything in
me sand he
collapsed on

IN SPITE OF HIS DANGLING PRONOUN

He was really her favorite
student, dark and just
back from the army with
hot olive eyes, telling her of
bars and the first
time he got a piece of
ass in Greece or was it
Italy and drunk on some strange
wine and she thought
in spite of his dangling
pronoun (being twenty-four and
never screwed but in her
soft nougat thighs) that he
would be a
lovely experience.
So she shaved her legs up high
and when he came
talking of footnotes she
locked him tight in her
snug black file cabinet where
she fed him twice a day and
hardly anyone noticed
how they lived among blue books
in the windowless office
rarely coming up for sun or the
change in his pronoun. Or the
rusty creaking chair
or that many years later
they were still going to town in
novels she never had time to finish

EATING THE RAIN UP

                gray Tuesday
        rain all night
        You said do you
                want to go
                        for cigarettes
                                do you want to

                        listen
                I've got a
        got a room we
                        could
        I've got something I want
        you
                at least
        we could
                        talk
                                tell me your name

        Books fell across the bed
        Your mustache
                        was the kind, I
                wrapped your mouth
            into me
                        yes I knew
                your thighs would be
        friendly, your
        hair closing
            down
                        small hands a pillow

                        and the
                wetness we grasped,
            that warm together

                        ate the rain up

LEMON SUN, SATURDAY

wind chimes

Jenny's slightly sour
sheets

the few white hairs on
your chest
I'm sorry I couldn't
forget
and swing, but my eyes
   were burning

lying now, this mattress
in your old friends' house

lemon sun, Billy's
TENNESSE BLUES
thru the shade. He's been

playing since midnight

Jenny standing in the
door, parting the
curtains slowly

LIGHT FROM THIS TURNING

I have lost touch with
distant trees,
the wind you brought
in your hair
and lilac hills.

Something different
bites into the river
and the river of lost days
floats over my tongue.

Love, you are like that
distant water, pulling
and twisting,
you turn me

apart from myself
like some frightening road,
something I don't want
to know.

Still, let my
hair float slow through
this new color,
let my eyes absorb
all light

from this turning
that has brought us
here, has carried us
to where we are,
we are

ON ANOTHER COAST

Maybe
could it have
been because of
rain that we fell
together so
easily that first time
rain keeping the
others near the
fire your hair was
blacker than the melon
seeds under the straw the towels
smelling of sweet trees our
bodies lifted to each other in the
rain cottage the
wet leaves pulling us
close and down

ALL AFTERNOON WE

read Lorca
by five snow
blurred the
glass. February. I
leaned against
those chill panes.
Gypsies
burned through the
snow with apples
You in the
other room
I was thinking
don't let
this be some
warmth I can
move near
and never know

LEMON WIND

all day
nobody wanted
to talk

the sleeping bags
were still wet
from the storm
in Chula Vista

Nothing went right.

But later the
wood we
burned had a sweet
unfamiliar smell

and all night
we could taste
lemons in the wind

NOT THINKING IT WAS SO WITH YELLOW FLOWERS

At night I
dreamed that
same dream,
the one
full of muscles
and thighs
that aren't you.
Later the fear
came back
crossing into
Mexico tho
at first
when I woke up
I thought it
wasn't true
the air was so
bright and
yellow flowers
were falling
from the
pepper tree
like suns

LUST BLOWING UNDER THE DOOR, BRIGHT AS STRAW

Your smile's like sun-
flowers he said
as tho
embarrassed his
hands were
pressing
awkwardly the
ring on his
second finger
close to her
eyes
from that room
a wheat sea
lust
blew under the
door bright
as straw
and his warm
parts on
her belly
those small
bones that changed her
small
bones to water
And not even
knowing
his name
until later
when the floor fell
the room
turned into a
painting
and the paint cracked

MUSTACHE

I was thinking
of it this
morning, those
marvelous hairs that
curl around your words

and how they smelled with
frost all over
in the mountains

And yes especially of that
time on the floor
looking like the
middle part of a thick
leggy bug I could

just see
above my belly, moist and
floating up
asked

is this
making your blood glow

EVEN THERE

It was December
and yes finally
you wanted me.
We ran down the
slick, narrow road.
Houses leaned
together the colors
wine and brown.
Remember the cracked
snow, our scarves
floating, getting
there out of
breath, our
hair melting.
Boots clicked under
the door. There
were quilts on the
sloped ceiling
and the old
stove you smiled
toward going to
heat up some
coffee. I kept
looking around
to get it right:
your suede jacket
hanging in several
places. Your
mouth was
corduroy I wanted
to touch
but even in the
dream, every
time I came
close to you
the place that was you
changed to air

IN VENICE, THAT NOVEMBER AND DECEMBER

17 cats ran in and
out windows that
never closed as Hare
Krishna jingled up
from Muscle Beach.
The house I stayed in
quieted by 4 in the
afternoon when every-
one left for work. I
curled in a stranger's
yellow terry cloth
robe as if to soak up
some sun color. I
hoped I'd be charmed
in tight jeans and fur
jacket, imagined them
sliced from my back,
butterfly wings, as
angels and truckers
howled *foxy* and pulled
up close enough to
touch my arms clutch-
ing a bottle of Chianti
or scotch I hoped
would help me flare
and glitter like some
blood sun the Pacific
gulps

VENICE DAPHNE RUN BACKWARDS

the way that sandpiper runs
as close to the water
and then knows, pulls
back, but not
before he's dug
into sea grass. I'm
walking out of branches,
wood, Daphne
ran backwards, my own
breakwater this time.
Blue shells, sun
cupped in the arm of some-
one who doesn't own
or want to own me.
The leaves he pulls from
my skin are stained
with the verbs of someone
who didn't see what she could.
Salt air chews them.
We dream of Nantucket,
wine in a gray wood
someday. You know I never
wanted a man just
for myself
but didn't know that.
Gulls. Old women
unbutton black coats,
feel the light, dreams moving
in their throats like birds.
They are willow roots
hanging on under
the sand, pushing deep.

In this light, if they
were to unloosen a few
pins they would grow into
their hair, birds blown in the
sun toward cities rarely
found on maps

TENTACLES, LEAVES

He saw my
picture in a
magazine and told
me he wanted
to take me down
the Mississippi
hollering poems and
blowing weed, he
sounded crazy
and I wrote that I'd
never been
beaten, that I was
a bitch.

He sent me
pain and lust
for 19 days, his
aloneness, how he
wanted to fall
into blue water.
He said my letters
fell apart
pressed to his
skin. In March
my arms started
melting and

I drank the
Château Ausone
he sent, by April
my face was
burning. He sent

me his so that in
Concord I could
just think about
him while the
river was
swelling

But I didn't
think he'd
come, writing back
checks, stealing
hamburg, staggering
with a torn suitcase and broken
shoes from California.
I didn't know where
to keep him

and I got drunk on
cognac before he
fell thru the
door

He taught me
what men did in
prison. His

eyes weren't mean
and blue when he said how
we would live in a
house of shells in
the ferns in
Big Sur
high on poems

he said we'd eat the
colors off Point
Lobos, dark
wine and succulents in
bed. I could
hear the
seals afternoons
we lay in a blur
of nutmeg
watching the curtains

his head on my
belly telling me about
women who
stopped mattering

that's when it
started getting
scary. One
waited five years after
getting a short
letter

I wouldn't even
take the bus
across town
tho I dreamed I'd go
with him
to Yugoslavia
and Mexico

he kept getting busted
and moved under the

stairs with
dead moths

drinking beer
and not coughing
Then he moved
out into
the trees

came leaf by
leaf in the morning

fog was what we
needed, a blur to
lie down and
lie in. I
never liked his
poems as
much as I
pretended, not
even the ones
he stole

but I loved the
stories, how he
made love in
coffins, stood
on the roof of his
house screaming
at stars.
But he kept
breaking into
places. Once

I held him 4 hours while
he cried

Next morning he poured chocolate
on my lips
and ate it and
talked about
going to Montana

we could live in a
wooden hut in
Canada with my cats

only nothing was
getting better
he vomited blood
and black things.
If he came in
late I thought
it was over

He'd just laugh.
We'd take a bottle
out into the
huge weeds
and collapse
laughing

other things fell
too, leaves
he'd slam into
chairs with
cigarettes, burn
holes in everything

I set the clock
ahead, wondered
how long this could
go on, the snow

coming and I
watered the mail
when he went to
get better

and didn't
by October I
couldn't move

whenever I went
there were
tentacles, his
eyes in the
window

I tripped on his
arms and then
cut out for Colorado

he couldn't just
stay in the
leaves, children
said he smelled
like fire

ladybugs lie on
their backs now the
wind is rising

I'm not
sorry that he
came

or that nothing
could keep him

SNOW FENCES, WORMWOOD

our room of
sun and metal

ghosts of Indians
the barns crumbling

wormwood inside us
only we didn't know

saw only the ice
cones dripping the

sheet's tangle smelling
good you said

as a woman had been there

MOVING BY TOUCH

that afternoon an
unreal amber
light 4 o'clock the
quietness of
oil February blue
bowls full of
oranges we were
spreading honey, butter
on new bread our
skin nearly
touching
Even the dark wood glowed

NICE

floating thru chairs
then opening
your hand
snakes in thru corduroy
my slip rides up the sun
makes the rug into a wool beach
sand assapples a wave of
thighs opening
skin prints a *V* on the rug your
knees go there
opening
and mouths suddenly too a
crack touch the pink smell
the sleek breathing flesh moans
a taste is nipples
bumping and your sail of blood
shove of bone tongue
traveling into this moist
lips opening the first bang of
hair and clothes rise from bodies
tremble the warm buttons rubbing
scratch of your mouth there
the damp nylon crotch
petals dissolving in a water my silk
hips you open and your fingers
under plunge so are pressing lips there
and your flesh
root shining
rocks your heat to my belly and my
legs spread so wide
greedy for the whole boat of you
in me your lovejuice dipping these
sloppy hills of cunt and you
put your good

hardness up me opening
skin rooms pounding
and circles slide your raw stem
my nails pull you
tighter
in and the slap of licked flesh oil
waves lunging and teeth
that eat everywhere ramming
the slit wet
opening and spread so
wide and splitting bite the sweet hot ache swell
your bomb breaking
too sucks the whole room up
fur zippersbeercans
and the sweat hair of groaning and sperm
till your cock bud throbs more
to ball me over and
again, better than summer
deep and nice
bringing everything
home

NOVEMBER 1 BOOGIE

on the third floor
rug rolled back
shoes under the sofa
toes instead of words
hair swinging like
Spanish moss in-
to a slow blues
kelp tangling in
water that shakes
hips and lips free
skin making love to
a whole room. No
wonder the Shakers
danced till they
couldn't stand,
went home with
grass stains,
starved

TWO THURSDAYS

we should have thought,
I could have been
sketching you all
this time

you tell me my
breasts are glistening,
take off the lilac
shirt and I lay there
hardly noticing mosquitoes,
the wool

If I say lie could I
lose this blue, could
I feel more like I
did then

thinking damp thoughts

the Chianti in an
old clay jar,
your cool shoulders

FROM THE MATTRESS ON THE FLOOR
UNDER THE FLAMING SKY PHOTOS

rain blurs moon
and dark, eyes dark
as licorice or water
in an old mine. A
stranger reading
Lorca in Spanish on
the phone. Later my
hands smelled like
him, cinnamon
skin. The dog barked
thru damp sheets.
I got wet, fingers
on my skin. *"You all
horned up."*
If I'd thought
twice I wouldn't
have in my leather
skirt and high
heels, pink *"What
are those,
barrettes?"* he
asked pulling rose
clips from my hair.
"And your scent," he was
pressing the strangest
flowers, pulled
my hair, tilted
forsythia dripping like
my hair, as I fell out
of what held me

GLASS

Oh, I was
wrong all that
time thinking I had the
glass tree inside
me, wanting to
slice it out before
splinters tore me
apart. I
thought I could
feel the crystal
branches press
holes from
inside

Do you know what
it's like to feel
that brittle?

Glass words
broke in my
mouth like that
boat on my
grandmother's
piano full of
bright beads.
When it
spilled, worms
slid out

I expected to
be that breakable,
growing hard,
something pressed inside
so long it crystallizes

I was waiting for the
edges to
crack thru my
skin

and I wanted to be
soft, to melt, a
lump of
snow in your
bed, water that
slid against
your hips

For years I woke up
imagining my
face froze.
I didn't understand
what comes from
living with a man who
can't get inside

I opened and the
cracks filled
with ice

Glass was all he could
give, expensive
glass rings
that might
cut my blood
forever,
2 clots
on a finger,

my thighs
were a glass
wishbone

But I
was lucky, he
pulled out

That night
tho I
slammed glass
until my face bled

red glass all over
the floor

The glass that
actually turned out
to be his heart
was unbreakable
of course

being a scientist
and really a
practical man

THE FIRST TIME

not in a marriage bed but
in a motel I could walk to
from that raised ranch my
husband and I played house
in. Virgins for years after
the wedding until I taunted
a man with words, the only
way I knew, got him to
slither in broken shoes from
another coast. I didn't know
if he really was an ex-con.
He looked like a stud. He
couldn't believe he had me
first, rocked back on his
knees in the motel as cars
honked by. I didn't know if
he could kill me, what I'd
get from him. Or that I
would not feel different,
would not feel much. I
looked in the mirror, felt
his tongue along my mouth.
Already I was longing for
quiet afternoons alone
while this large man who
wouldn't fit anywhere
slogged a beer, grinned,
said he kept tasting me

JUST AFTER FORSYTHIA, AFTER ICED RAIN

Rattlesnake Mountain
pokes up thru the clouds
and we drive past pastures
and tangled orchards.
Trees squeak, green fur
in the wind sounds like
dolphins calling. Above
a field of trillium, the
Liz Taylor of wild flowers,
a nipple hill of snow
dotted with mayapple
and bloodroot. Indians
used it for war paint.
Wintergreen we pick for
tea. Deerberries and
yellow lady slippers. In
this quilt of pastels, I
think of what the blind
would smell, the musky
damp wood, the earth
opening. I think of those
on the island where no
one sees in color seeing
70 shades of gray in
the leaves and as the
light goes, the glint and
shimmer, the texture of
petals in near darkness

THE CHILD WE WILL NOT HAVE

Will be a boy. Dean Michael
will go to law school and play
football. I'll listen to September
get loud and then quieter,
sneak into the smallest room

to write SOS notes in returnable soda
bottles, my belly crinkled as the toenail
that falls off after a torturous summer
of pointe. This child you always wanted
swims in my arms like that gone nail,

I talk to it with my mouth shut. It teaches
you to sign, lips reads my nipples. In the movie
of September, some of the stills are missing.
I clutch the baby like someone at a crash site,

hear glass fall. The child we will not have
is all we wanted, all that holds us together

HE SAID IN THE HOSPITAL IT

isn't much like
you'd imagine
they're joking
paraplegics putting
on rock n roll
loud to bug some dudes
who just like *Aida.*
We were glad to be
coming out of the jungle,
not in body bags.
First day out with my
new leg and I think I'm
hot stuff, don't know its
got this spring-loaded
thing and I twist on
a bar stool and my
leg spits and flings
itself out, yanks a
briefcase of this
man's arm and throws it
across the floor. He
gives me a funny look.
Then once one foot
turned around so
I looked to be
walking backward and
forward and a kid
pointed it out
and said *look at that*
man as his mama was
hushing. *You'd be*
surprised what I can
do with it. But,
Honey, there are
some things it's more
comfortable to
take it off for

AFTERNOONS IN THE BLUE RAIN

When I still wondered
if you'd call. Now
those Junes, a cake
of soap made out of
flesh, a lampshade you
can see where a
nipple or tendon
was. I'll wait
in the dark for the
ice you left plunged
in me like a mugger's
knife to melt into
the Hudson River. First
I thought your heart was
in your penis. Now I
can see it was in
the leg you saw
torn from you
on the other side of the
road, Vietnam.

KISS, BABY, THE NEW FILM

a much more rare obsession than mine, tho
in some ways, not that different. The woman
in love with what's dead, what's given up
on breathing, caring, could be me knocking
my knuckles raw on your metal door while
you gulp another beer, put your head down
on the table. With you, it often was like
singing to someone in a casket the lid was
already down on, still expecting something.
She buried animals in the woods, didn't mind
touching them. Though I made our nights into
something more, I could have been coiled
close to a corpse. No, that part is a lie. Your
body was still warm. It was everything inside
where your heart must have been that was
rigid, ice. The woman in the film went to work,
an embalming assistant. Isn't that what I'm
doing? Keeping you with words? Embracing
you on the sheet of this paper, a tentative
kiss on cold lips, the cuddling of cadavers?
In the film, the woman says loving the dead is
"like looking into the sun without going blind,
is like diving into a lake, sudden cold, then
silence." She says it was addictive. I know about
the cold and quiet afterward, how you were a drug.
If she was spellbound by the dead, who
would say I wasn't, trying to revive, resuscitate
someone not alive who couldn't feel or care
with only the shell of the body. Here, where no-
body can see, I could be licking your dead body
driving thru a car wash. I could be whispering
to the man across the aisle, "bodies are addictive."
Our word for the loved and the dead are the same,
the beloved, and once you had either while you
have them, you don't need any other living people
in your life

NOW YOU'VE SPENT A WHOLE MONTH IN THE GROUND

past muscle memory.
In ballet some way
tendons and sinews
move are like a
computer whose
files won't erase.
Phantom pain, an
old story. But what
of the tissues that
connected to what
was gone, a leg
exploding across a
minefield, there
and not there like
a lover who says its
not you and dissolves.
With you, I was like
a Siamese twin who
survives the other
but never heals, burns,
stays raw where the
hearts and lungs
connected

WHITE TREES IN THE DISTANCE

a white wind of
petals, maybe snow.
The longest I've
been so close to
you on the sheet
of paper. Like your
death, these poems
about you, a wild
surprise. The last
page in the note-
book, still I think
I'll need another
notebook before I
can let you go

A WOMAN GOES INTO THE CEMETERY

disappears behind granite
and is never heard from
again. We don't quite
believe this. She could
have gone to the museum
or called her girlfriend
to meet her for lunch
but instead took the
metro to the cemetery
as if to lie down with the
dead one who always said
her lips brought him
back to life. It was a warm
day for December even
tho it was the day of
the least light. She was
wearing the denim mini
I had in my closet,
her hair almost as long
and red as mine. Some might
suppose I'm that woman,
it seems there are clues.
But listen, the buried
man was already dead to
me before he slept
under the grave in this
city and the me who would
have banged myself
raw on his metal
door had already grown
skin too thick to feel

BLUE SUNDAY

imagining that he slips
from her the way rings
do from a finger in
the cold. Leaves. October,
black spots on the mirror.
Separation blues in the
bed. Touching his shoulders
here on paper, he's like
all the flowers that I
draw, bright wild petals
that don't connect to
any stem

THE AFFAIR

The margaritas were blue with paper roses.
Later I thought how they were the only salt of those nights.
His e mail letters like skin,
very taut. What he didn't say drugged me.
Language was wild, intense.
I could feel him, his screen name a tongue.
Verbs taut, what he didn't say a drug.
It was a dangerous tango.
I wanted his body glued to mine.
Distance kept the electricity vivid.
It was a dangerous tango.
How could I know his mother leaped into Niagara Falls?
I fell for his words, what he left out.
How could I know he was ice.
How could I know his mother leaped into the falls.
Even in the heat, he was icy.
His name was Snow. Our last night
we drove thru fog until 3.
He told me things he said he'd never told anyone.
My thigh burned where it touched him.
On our last night we drove thru Austin
mist talking. I was burning.
He photographed me, exhausted, at 3 a.m. Everything he
told me was a scar. My hair curled in a way
I hated. After that night I wasn't sure
I would be pretty again.
Everything he told me was a
scar. Under the ice the anger in him was lava.
I wanted him, always longing for men
with something missing.
The margaritas were the only salt I'd taste.
The anger in him was lava under the ice.
I wanted more, my longing a scar.
When he didn't write, I printed his old e-mail.
When I no longer looked for it
his e-mail was there, like a mugger.
The margaritas were strong with black paper roses

WHEN I WAS NO LONGER MY LEATHER JACKET

something he'd picked up
and gently carried to the
closet. When I was no
longer something he half
wanted to wear, held so
delicately, smiled at like
when he came in later to
the reading, said he would
have brought the margarita
but he didn't know if I
liked it on the rocks, how I
felt about salt. Before I
was no longer my jacket,
darkly mysterious, soft but
with a musky smell, flexible
enough to do what he
wanted with. Before that I
was all animal, wild. I was prey
he was on a safari for, caught
in his crosshairs. He could
taste my hair thru e-mail.
Once he tracked me as far as
San Antonio, couldn't
find me. This time I was the
lure, the flash of a few verbs and
he cancelled classes, took off
work. I was something he
couldn't stroke like the leather.
He was used to things being
fatal, leaps and cracks. He was
a journalist, wanted no
emotion to get in the way
of the facts

AFTER 9 DAYS OF COLD RAIN, ANYTHING BLOOMING TRAMPLED

"Still west," you write, "with a PO
box in Hell." A jolt, like the wild pear
exploding hours after Sunday snow.
White crystals, white petals. "On

the tip of the spear," you said. "Hard
to unplug, wired for weeks, dreams
like war games. The green of your
words out-jades the geranium. A

jolt, your words after almost a year.
Not even the spears of pink leaves
I could smell from the road as much
comfort. "Might be in your city,"

Darvan, codeine—warm as the cat
coiled in my knees. "Still west," you
wrote. Then you didn't. War dreams
hang in branches. I think maybe

Jakarta, he wrote me once from there.
The geranium that should have died
spreads thru the sunroom. Last year's
oak leaves hang on the branches. The

petals I smelled from the road smashed
into mud. Pink spears gone, the tips
of the spears he wrote about dissolve.
Rain, the branches, pink lace over, I

watch for his screen name. I was over
that. The cherries are over, the nine
days of cold rain aren't, the paper
says, over yet

IN A NOTEBOOK FROM PARIS

scraps, the handwriting
that had sloped in the
yellow light of Florence
toward where each line
was heading, now almost
too real with its *this
is impossible* under a
line from the man sing-
ing near Rue de la Harpe,
moaning *where do I go
from here.* I said I
didn't know how to
change anything. How
little I knew. And then
the spit out, leaning
backward like trees
squashed toward the
left by monsoon winds,
I feel dead, dead,
darkly underlined

HAVING YOU COME UP AFTER SO MUCH TIME

thinking what it
would be like re-
reading your letter
like a map, I folded
September, then un-
folded it again. I
thought I was
ready but it was
like thunder you
hear on the phone
when you're talking
to someone where
the storm is. You
know it's coming,
moving east like
most weather but
you still wake up
startled, dazed.
When it breaks, the
rain on the glass,
the lightning that
makes the room
even darker

READING THOSE POEMS BECAUSE I CAN'T GET STARTED THINKING OF THE PHONE CALL THAT CAME, THAT YOU MIGHT

before I get to the
end of the line, my
head's milkweed.
Something in me
drifts out into the
trees thru the
stained glass, my
black seeds flying
out to where you
say we'll find
columbine. They
get hung up in the
leaves, words sinking
in where they can't
grow like what
was starting to
in the shot deer
left in the
snow all winter

KNOCKOUT BALLROOM

a concussion nearly,
slamming down the floor
in a wild jive. He knocked
me out and kept doing
it. No wonder the blue
inside leaked out, stained
fingers and wrists. Like
the sound of geese in
flight, I can't forget the
touch of his skin on my
arms. But that's a lie.
The studio's so cold skin's
hard to get to. But I will
tell you that in that ice,
forget the ice inside me,
I could have gladly stayed
frozen in a silver tango,
my legs locked in his, to
an ice sculpture

LATE WINTER SNOW

when cold ice fell
on everything as frigid
I knew the stains would
never come out. Under
what lost all color I
expected hyacinths,
crocus to bloom but no,
you ruined the night.
There was nothing
filling the room with
sweetness. The one I
couldn't touch did the
Viennese waltz under
spotlights while I
sat, stone in a dark cove
of the club. Snow grey
past the velvet curtain.
I wanted to be out of
there, your words bullets.
Amazing blood didn't
pool around my legs.
It didn't matter that
what stung would melt.
It didn't matter

TODAY ON THE METRO

he could have been
that Persian vase
that grabbed me. I
was walking fast
past the shop named
Ecstasy. I know if
I don't go back for
that dark blue rose,
I may never see it
again. In a day, it is
gone. He is like that
vase. I don't need him,
have no place for
him in my life but
when I see him whirl
by on the dance floor,
like a boat, ghostly
in fog with that vase
on its deck, loss
explodes. This ache
for something that
never was mine,
that Persian vase, so
like another love
left me notes for in
his house. He is some
thing glimpsed in
a window, his words,
like the canals and
alleys of a foreign
place I'm wild to go
back to. Or the bolero
music drifting in

rose leaves if the wind
is right to seduce
me back to the paid-
for hour with him,
running towards and
away from what, if
I had it, it would be-
come something else

THOSE NIGHTS

branches across the
clouds could have
been antlers. Of
course they were
just trees. Arms

were arms. You
were dark as your
hair, blue as your
sea eyes. It was
not always like

talking to some-
one in a coffin.
Your stories
wrapped me in
green like grape

leaves. Afterwards,
it was often like
having a beautiful
dress, pale lace
tangling at my feet

so I couldn't move

GOING HOME

(family)

I THINK OF MY GRANDFATHER

on a cramped ship
headed toward Ellis Island.
Fog, foghorns for a
lullaby. The black
pines, a frozen pear.
Straw roofs on fire.
If there were postcards
from the sea there might
have been a Dear
Hannah or Mama, hand-
colored with salt.
I will come and get you.
If the branches are
green, pick the apples.
When I write next, I will
have a pack on my
back, string and tin.
I dream about the snow
in the mountains. I never
liked it but I dream of
you tying a scarf
around my hair, your
words that white dust

IF MY GRANDMOTHER COULD HAVE WRITTEN A POSTCARD TO THE SISTER LEFT BEHIND

It would be written
on sand, or on a
hand-colored photo-
graph of a country
with nobody waiting
with guns, no thatched
roofs on fire, no
hiding in trees after
a knock on the
door: *Sister, it is*
nothing like we had
or what we imagined.
There are no Jews
in the small rural
towns hardly. They
don't spit or say
we are thieves but
it is as icy in Vermont
as days in Russia.
Lake Champlain is
not like our sea. We
are safe, we are
lonely

IF MY GRANDMOTHER WOULD HAVE WRITTEN A POSTCARD TO ODESSA

she would write her
name in salt, salt
and mist, an SOS
from the ship sea
wind slaps with night
water. *Somehow I'm
dreaming of Russian
pines. I don't dream
of the houses on fire,
babies pressed into
a shivering woman's
chest to keep them
still. Someone had
something to eat the
color of sun going
down behind the
hill late summer,
rose, with its own
sweet skin. They
are everywhere in
America. If the lilies
bloom in our
town of darkness,
just one petal in an
envelope would be
enough*

FROM THE FIRST WEEKS IN NEW YORK, IF MY GRANDFATHER COULD HAVE WRITTEN A POSTCARD

if he had the words, the
language. If he could
spell. If he wasn't
selling pencils but knew
how to use them, make
the shapes for words
he doesn't know. If he
was not weighed down
with a pack that made
red marks on his shoulder,
rubbed the skin that
grew pale under layers
of wet wool, he might have
taken the brown wrapping
paper and tried to write
three lines in Russian
to a mother or aunt he
might never see again.
But instead, too tired to
wash hair smelling of
burning leaves he walked
thru, maybe he curled
in a blue quilt, all he had
of the cottage he left
that night running past
straw roofs on fire,
dreamt of those tall black
pines, but not how, not
yet 17, he will live in
a house he will own,
more grand than any he
saw in his old country

56 NORTH PLEASANT STREET

past the beads hung over the door,
rose light floods the back room
where the safe is, my grandmother
with a sick baby crying, tapping
the pane under apple leaves

My mother is 8, her new doll's
head lies smashed on the floor.
She is hating her brother. Spirea
covers the sidewalk. She is
furious at her brother and runs
into the hot stove. Her

grandmother gets a cold knife.
My mother screams, is sure the
knife is a weapon. She is wild
to claw her brother. My great
grandmother will die without
replacing the broken head tho

she promises this until her last
month in the blue bed where I
will try to sleep when my mother
goes to have my sister and won't
tho my grandmother sings

The White Cliffs of Dover and the
apples are like magic green eggs
in July light behind the house

AFTER THE VISIT

flat blue hills

yellow light.
November in the
old house. The

walls pull from
the floor, she
barely knows me
or my voice. Stained

Chinese carpet.
My grandmother
wrapped in blue sheets

on the chair where
her old man sat

and stopped her
from singing 60
years, now under
the blanket in
her own dark

singing *you are
my* the midnight
leaves, her arms
growing smaller
sunshine my only

ESTELLE, STAR STONES

That summer on the sea porch, Winthrop, was
it July? My sister crying. Estelle,
even your name a bracelet, star stones

stars I put on and let the dark waves crash
on the bed. We were drifting into your 19-year-
old life, imagining your boyfriends on the
other edge of your skin. Nipples on the beach, your

tan. You brought blue bowls of raspberries,
cream fingers. Estelle, Estelle, you wanted
to be what your name was and sang weekends on
the radio, sang brushing my hair in the
bathroom light. The white tiles cool.
My sun burnt skin. You said

you'd never stop singing, wouldn't marry and
hummed something that both our fathers heard
on that boat from Lithuania, heard in a
strange tongue. We couldn't understand
you said but would later and how
you'd dance as those children
had. Black pines.

Russia glowing in the sea. Night. We were
wrapped in cats and velvet. Moon on
the stones. You told us of dreams hidden
in the stone, got out that—I remember
the gold around the latch—

jewel box, it was what went with wishes
in old books and moonstones. Dream
fur. Choose one for later.

The smoothest stones. Your long, thick hair.
Goodnight. Your name a charm still
though you married in some split-level,
your throat stuffed with china
and none of the things you
promised would happen happened

THE COUSIN'S PARTY

A Sunday every August my mother's cousins
came with photographs from summers they
camped out on North Pleasant, my grand-
mother making lemon meringue pie my mother
ordered in restaurants, always found wanting.
The last time I drove up, a lover's scent
still in my hair, my lace smelling of him,

leaves tipped with red. Suddenly, the cousins
began to go, my mother couldn't swallow.
Someone went into the hospital for something
minor but didn't return. Kay, who loved my
poems, had fought so many parts of her being
poked at and sliced away but always made up
—with a new wig, smiling and dancing,

suddenly couldn't go on anymore. They skipped
the party for one year while another cousin fell
and couldn't remember his name and Kay's husband,
always her lover, the one she talked about putting on
sexy lingerie for even while having chemo, wore
a wig to go to sleep, falls over in a day and uncles
start coughing, gasping for air they never get again.

Like birds migrating as if they got a signal, some
radar, or something in the leaves and they're on
their way, like they did other summers, packing the
old Ford for Atlantic City, Chicago World's Fair 1933
in panama hats and Navy middy dresses, everyone
going, not wanting to be left behind

MY FATHER TELLS US ABOUT LEAVING VILNIUS

On the night we left Vilnius, I had to bring goats
next door in the moon. Since I was not the youngest, I
couldn't wait pressed under a shawl of coarse cotton
close to Mama's breast as she whispered "hurry" in Yiddish.
Her ankles were swollen from ten babies. Though she was
only thirty her waist was thick, her lank hair hung in

strings under the babushka she swore she would burn
in New York City. She dreamt others pointed and snickered
near the tenement, that a neighbor borrowed the only bowl
she brought that was her mother's and broke it. That night
every move had to be secret. In rooms there was no heat in,
no one put on muddy shoes or talked. It was forbidden to leave,

a law we broke like the skin of ice on pails of milk. Years from
then a daughter would write that I didn't have a word for
America yet, that night of a new moon. Mother pressed my
brother to her, warned everyone even the babies must not make
a sound. Frozen branches creaked. I shivered at men with
guns near straw roofs on fire. It took our old samovar, every

coin to bribe someone to take us to the train. "Pretend to be
sleeping," father whispered as the conductor moved near. Mother
stuffed cotton in the baby's mouth. She held the mortar and
pestle wrapped in my quilt of feathers closer, told me I would
sleep in this soft blue in the years ahead. But that night I
was knocked sideways into ribs of the boat so seasick I
couldn't swallow the orange someone threw from an upstairs
bunk tho it was bright as sun and smelled of a new country I
could only imagine though never how my mother would become
a stranger to herself there, forget why we risked dogs and guns to come

PHOTOGRAPH

My father sister and
I in the trees with
our hair blowing. My
sister as usual has
something in her
hands and grins in
a way no one could
say no to, dancing
in restaurants
until she pulls in
to herself at 19
like the turtles
she collects. But
here she's the sweet
pouter, my father's
pockets bulge with
things, the gum
he'll give us in
the brown chair
later reading the
funnies. I've got
a little pot and
my arms are heavy,
my father touches
us both lightly
as if he's not
sure we're real

THE OTHER FATHERS

would be coming back
from some war, sending
back stuffed birds or
handkerchief in navy
blue with *Love* painted
on it. Some sent telegrams
for birthdays, the pastel
letters like jewels. The
magazines for children
were full of fathers who
were doing what had
to be done, were serving,
were brave. Someone
yelped there'd be confetti
in the streets, maybe
no school. That soon
we'd have bananas. My
father sat in the gray
chair, war after war,
hardly said a word. I
wished he had gone
away with the others
so maybe he would
be coming back to us

MY SISTER WANTS ME TO COME AND READ THROUGH THIRTY YEARS OF DIARIES

in the house overlooking
rain-bent pines,
in the life others
would envy she loses her-
self in fragments. *How
could we have changed so*
she asks over the
phone. *How could I not*
still be eleven in front
of the old Plymouth
on Main street,
Mother younger there
than I am now. Beginnings.
What might go, pressed
flat as a daisy from
someone she tries to
remember like a deaf
man remembering an
opera he heard
eleven years ago.
My sister, fragile, as
in demand as those flowers,
has found her days
losing color, turning thin,
breakable as those nearly
transparent brittle leaves.
Nothing bends
like the pines. Her
days are a shelf of
blown glass buds
a heartbeat could shatter. *Come*
she says *We can laugh*

at what seemed so
serious then. Maybe from
what happened in the
apartment when the
roof fell in or
at Nanny's as Herbert
was dying we can
know something about
the stories we
haven't begun yet

THE CAT'S YELP IN BLACK LIGHT

Pine needles dripping,
covering cars deeper than
mist. My sister is pulled
toward what tore night
like a child in pain
to where the cat drags
one half of his body
thrashing and tangling
through legs of chairs
no light's touched.
We wrapped his
writhing in flannel,
drove on winding roads
thru maple hills,
reaching toward noon.
Nothing to do but wait.
We were shaking, numb,
bought butter pecan
ice cream that dripped
down skin like tears.
Embolism. White pines
blackening. Next
morning the vet says
the cat died in the
night. A sack of clots,
a whole heart-full. My
sister doesn't stop
clearing the table,
packs the car, it's as
if the cat's wet fur
and twitching have
moved inside her

MY SISTER SAYS BUT DOESN'T *EVERYONE* WASTE THEIR LIFE?

as Mother shrivels, as her
kingdom reaches only to the
nightstand, to arranging the
way her slippers point. "So

full of the joy of life"
someone wrote in her college
yearbook, maybe why she named
her second child Joy. Maybe

she felt it slipping from
her. My sister, blonde,
the pretty one with
boys giving her roses

and watches, now sinks
back into her shell like
those turtles she cages,
covers windows to keep

out light. She reminds me
of our mother, sitting
in darkness with a
cigarette, waiting for

my call, expecting the
worst. My sister and I
chose to have cats
instead of children

We feared becoming
what we clawed at and
bit to move away from,
as if we could help

keep genes hostage,
howling at each other
like animals caught in
traps they'd gnaw

their own legs off to escape

READING THE POEM SHE WROTE THAT I HADN'T

I didn't know she
watched men watch
me walking, thought
I was beautiful

When we kiss she
wrote we come close
but we kiss air.
I haven't seen her

for seven years. I
never read the poem
about sleeping together
in the lake house

before my wedding,
never heard her say
"I want to put my
arms around Lyn

and kiss the
skin from her"

MY SISTER, RE-READING 32 YEARS OF DIARIES

not like the book of
life where deaths and births
are sealed but a film
run backward, a woman
pulling away from
arms and lips and skin,
letting go, swirling
backward, curled as
an embryo, she locks her-
self in the bathroom
apartment of stained lilac
as water crashes against
ragged stone. The black
pines bend over like my
sister in the dark room in
the rain. She is 36, 18, 8,
becoming thinner, laughing.
The pages open like a rose,
the words a rose pressed
on a night moon licked her
skin, translucent as her
long blonde hair. From here,
that nymph is a stranger.
Like the rose, the words
lose their color, spaces
fill with blurred nights. But
the leaves, fragile and thin,
ghosts of what was,
smell of something lush in
darkness. In the rain my
sister curls into the quilt
made of time and loss,
pulls the past as far into
Junes to come as she can

IN REXALL'S, MIDDLEBURY

the dark booth held us like a cove.
My mother put on high heels and lipstick.
Fruit parfait in glasses, a sweetness.
A comfort to eavesdrop on the others talking.

My mother put on high heels and lipstick.
My father never cared if we had a real house
where my sister and I wouldn't be ashamed to bring friends.
In the dark of the booth, I could imagine, someday, being a beauty.

My father never cared if we had a real house.
My mother never wanted to come back to this town she eloped to escape.
She went out with realtors for 15 years.
In her last weeks she said if she could go anywhere she would pick New York City

My mother never wanted to come back to this town,
imagined the bustle of cities, the theater, the subway.
My father sat in the yellow chair, read the *Wall Street Journal* without talking.
My mother played gipsy music and Cab Calloway, "Raisins and Almonds"

I imagined the bustle of cities
where what happened mattered.
My father sat in the yellow chair, quiet as stones.
Bits of my mother's red lipstick swirled in fruit parfait.
The dark booth held us like a cove

THE DEEPER YOU GO

(mother)

PHOTOGRAPHS OF MOTHERS AND DAUGHTERS

you can almost always
see the mother's hands

the daughter usually
nests in a curve of
the mother's hair or
neck like it was a cave

the way cats do the
night it starts to snow

Some seem to suck
on the mother's breath.
You might think the
mother had eyes
in her fingers

Often her hands
are on the daughter's
shoulders, pulling
her close, as if

she wanted to press
her back inside

23 HILL STREET

Something dark was moving
toward Europe that year they
moved into the flat on the hill.
My father worked in his rich
brother's store, stopped reading
or saying much. It was gradual.
My mother didn't say a thing,
sat on her side of the black
Plymouth thinking maybe
of the men she didn't,
wouldn't. Thinking never.
Whispers of war burned thru
their sleep, were in the park
where you could say something
and the rumors went to other
people's houses. Everyone
wore gray. Buildings, a
whole town the color of
granite. And the dim light
in the Brown Derby where they
went to drink beer that whole
spring waiting for me as
bright, as warm as they'd be
for a while

THERE WERE SPIDERS OVER THE CARRIAGE

I don't remember.
My mother weighed
120, had bad dreams
of war. She took
money her mother
sent for clothes,
bought pots and
pans. Somewhere
across town my
father was flirting
in the Brown Derby
while she read about
leftovers, whispered
on the round stone
bench, "Merle doesn't
have to live like
this," heard the
words echo as loud
behind her almost
as a gun exploding

38 MAIN STREET

sitting on the toilet
with you in the tub,
Mommy, Frieda May.
The blue room like water.
Smell of wet clothes
and talcum. You never
liked your name. Ben
couldn't come in.
Sitting on the toilet,
your breasts floating
on the water, you
younger than I
am now

MORE MOTHER AND DAUGHTER
PHOTOGRAPHS

My mother and sister
near an old black seventies
Chevy. My sister in a
nest between my mother's
arms. You can just see
certain parts of my mother,
like a branch in a backdrop.
I'm in several with
her, standing in back, her
arms around me, her prize
melon, a book just she
would write. I remember
the rabbi said enjoy
your wedding, after that
it will be your husband
and your child. I've
noticed this in several
other photos of mothers
with their girls, the
daughter held up close in
front like someone with
a desperate sign, words
pointing west or saying
Hartford. The daughter
almost blots the mother
out. It's as if there
was some huge dark hole
only a camera would pick
up where something that
had got away had been

MY MOTHER AND THE MATCHES

She said *I didn't know you*
couldn't either. My mother,
who knew which man was
circumcised and which
woman's laugh I liked

Light matches? No, we both
laugh, we couldn't. I
nearly flunked chemistry.
One day when my lab partner
didn't come, the Bunsen
burner stayed unlit

At Raven's I mangle four
boxes of matches and
can't admit I'm afraid
to be burned

I spent a whole year
dreaming of fires, my
mother up April nights
sniffing for smoke. She

once said *You mean you'd*
swallow it? But she never,
until this morning, talked
about *her* fear of matches,

startling as knowing she
has a down quilt from
Odessa in a closet I've
never seen. I tell her

I never lit a candle until
lights went out for two days
in a blue cabin in Maine
and then I lit it on the wood

stove that had to be kept
burning. I hardly slept. *And
do you hate to kill flies?*
my mother asks, like Columbus
discovering a new continent

MY MOTHER AND THE BED

No, not that way she'd
say when I was 7, pulling
the bottom sheet smooth,
you've got to, saying
hospital corners

I wet the bed much later
than I should, until
just writing this, I
hadn't thought of
the connection

My mother would never
sleep on sheets someone
else had. I never
saw any stains on hers
though her bedroom was

a maze of powder, hair-
pins, black dresses.
Sometimes she brings her
own sheets to my house,
carries toilet seat covers.

Lyn, did anybody sleep
in my, she always asks.
Her sheets, her hair
smell of smoke. She
says the rooms here
smell funny

We drive at 3 a.m.
slow into Boston and
strip what looks like
two clean beds as the
sky gets light. I

smooth on the form-
fitted flower bottom.
She redoes it.

She thinks of my life
as a bed only she
can make right

MY MOTHER AND I WERE

the closest, but we
had the most violent
fights: clawing and
screaming down the long
dark hall with peeling
Chinese red figures.
I hit her in the car. No
man's ever slapped
me, my father never
lifted a belt but my
mother and I hurled
fists and words at each
other. Last week Ester
said *you mean you
really said fuck off to
your mother in public?*
In the apartment the
doors were dark and
thick when they slammed.
I told her things I
knew she'd hate: about
the night in the motel
when it almost happened
and how I sneaked out
of the sorority house.
She called me slut
all the way up Rt. 7,
told my uncles not to
give me a car. I
sharpened my claws on
her until they were
too sharp to use. Each
time we leave each other
it hurts. But before that
there's the broken nails,
the things we can't
say to anybody else

IN THE DREAM

My mother says look,
I'll show you why I
can't go to the party
tonight, takes off
her blouse, back
toward me. I see no-
thing, a dime sized
bump I never would
have noticed with a
cut across it. My
mother, who never
complained, cooked
venison when the
hurricane blew a
roof off a friend's
house and thirteen
people slept in our
beds the day some-
thing was cut out
of her, blood still
dripping. My mother
who could open jars
no one else could,
who never stayed in
bed one day, says
the small circle
hurts. I press her
close, terrified
I'm losing what
I don't know

MY MOTHER'S ADDRESS BOOK

With rubber bands
flecked with powder,
slack as the face of
a child who won't
eat. Almost half
the names crossed
out with a line,
Buzzy darkened over
with a pencil, as if there
was a rush like some-
one throwing a dead
relative's shoes and
wool dresses toward
the Salvation Army
baskets, someone
catching a train,
breathless, the
graphite black as
shining freight

MY MOTHER STRAIGHTENING POTS AND PANS

"I can't see why you
keep so many coffee pots
with cracked handles,"
she frowns as if looking
at a police lineup
where all the faces
were lovers who'd
slid thru my arms.
"You've got a lot of
junk but nothing
to make something hearty.
You need pots that
would last a life.
They don't make pots
or men as they used to"

BARNSTABLE, TWO YEARS AGO

reeds and marsh
grass, a frozen gray.
The cat locked in one
room at Murray's,
we walked, my mother
with more energy than
she'll have again
along Route 1 to the
only restaurant.
Torn branches,
litter of broken
glass. We had to
yell to hear each
other over cars,
bitching, laughing
feeling sun thru
winter coats

EARLY FRIDAY I WONDERED, SUDDENLY, WAS CAB CALLOWAY LIVING, WAS HE DEAD

leaped to the Boardwalk where my mother had us
waiting in line for a chance to see his
crinkly *Hi De Ho* laugh tho my sister and I
wanted to feel the salt wind lick us like
sailors' eyes, safe in the leash of our
mother's sighs no matter how tight my sarong

dress of aqua and jade leaves like one my
mother would pick out when she couldn't
still walk, let alone think of shimmying to
Minnie the Moocher, only got it after making
me try it on saying she couldn't even be buried
in it. Salt wind and lights like rhinestones

and diamond as unlike the room she left when
she was hostage to my sister's bossiness, *her*
perfect body, tiny and blonde as we grew like
flowers my mother over-watered, wild to make
sure nothing died, now spreading beyond even her
biggest clothes as she plotted to keep the sun-

dress she could never wear that July when she
helped my mother out on an ambulance ride south.
But that June we were teens, my sister wrapped
in dreams of races and jockeys like Willie Shoe-
maker and I in my even smaller sleek clothes
were herded in to hear this man who wiggled as much
as Elvis. Our mother's hair, black fire shaking, maybe
46 or 47—too old we figured then to be so taken by Cab's
flirty eyes, his scat hinting at what *our* mother couldn't
imagine we were sure, let alone want

MY MOTHER'S THIRD CALL ON A DAY OF SLEET AND DECEMBER FALLING

as if the whiteness was
gauze wrapped over the
mouth of someone dying
and she had to slash it
with a last word, or
Monday was a blank
sheet of paper only my
words would cling to.
My mother who lugged
suitcases with me in the
'78 blizzard when subways
broke in Brooklyn, says
the wind crossing the
street wouldn't let
her breathe. I'm stand-
ing with my hair dripping,
turning the quilt darker
blue, the water boiling
downstairs, thinking how
long it's been since I've
gone to visit her. Or
haven't told her I had
to rush but just let the
words between us wrap
us like the navy afghan
on the velvet couch with
the stain where the gray
cat peed and just drifted
in the closeness, linked
as we once were as if
we always would be

MY MOTHER LISTENS TO CLASSICAL MUSIC

As she didn't
always, preferring
talk radio. Schubert,
and Bizet, Chopin,
as if words were
too charged, now
too hard to hold
onto. Minor notes
in Bloch soothe,
a hand on a burning
forehead. I like
the wash of adagios,
what's moving slow,
stretching, not
jarring as so
much is lately. You
can take this
radio my mother
says, it gets TV.
I don't want it I
say, lying there
with notebook and
paper and she says
"not now, after
I'm gone."

GETTING MY MOTHER ICE

Nothing lasts long
in this heat
except the dark
of waiting. At
2 a.m. or 3 or
4 I lead her
like a child
with a night-
mare to the
bathroom across
the hall. If I
don't get the
washcloth
right, not too
wet, or hot
or soapy, she
will refuse
Demerol, lie
moaning, *I
can't*. It
seems those
words are
my words

MY MOTHER WANTS LAMB CHOPS, STEAKS, LOBSTER, ROAST BEEF

something to get
her teeth in.
Forget the shakes
cancer patients
are supposed to
choose, forget
tapioca pudding,
vanilla ice,
she wants what
is full of blood,
something to
chew to get
the red color
out of, something
she can attack
fiercely. My
mother, who never
was namby-pamby,
never held her
tongue, never
didn't attack
or answer back,
worry about
angering or hurt-
ing anybody but
said what she
felt and wouldn't
walk any tight-
rope, refuses the
pale and delicate
for what's blood,
what she can
chew, even spit
out if she
needs
to

THE YAHRTZEIT LIGHT

Dusty, with some skeletons of
a flying thing that died
in it, as if the flame
already had been pulling
on things restless and alive.
My mother bought it, an
extra one, the year after
my grandmother died,
when my mother's hair was
still dark and curly. It
waited fifteen years in the
middle of scales, shoe
polish and liquids to make
what is glowing hot, spit
eerie light and the flicker
of death into shadows. I
couldn't throw it out:
more Jewish than anything
I owned and wondered if my
mother would have other
people leaving too fast to
say goodbye to, rub her
hands in front of this
candle, rub what was still
warm numb as a heart rubbed
raw. This morning, my mother
at ninety pounds, was afraid to
stay alone in the mall,
her face gray as the stone
squares she had trouble,

even holding my arm, getting
across. I take her bag, as
if alone she might collapse
and nobody would know who
she was to claim her. My
uncle's voice on tape
reminds it's the anniversary
of my mother's mother's death
so tonight I give the candle
to her, go down to the room
where no candle could catch.
In the glitz of fire, my
mother's cheeks are caverns
no light fills

MINT LEAVES AT YADDO

In frosty glasses of
tea. Here, iced
tea is what we
make waiting for

death with this
machine my mother
wanted. Not knowing
if she'd still be

here for her birth-
day we still shopped
madly, bought her

this iced tea maker for.

For twenty days my
mother shows only
lukewarm interest
in presents or tea,

vomits even water,
but I unpack the
plastic, intent
on trying this

sleek device while
my mother, queen
of gadgets—
even a gun to

demolish flies—
maybe the strangest
thing she got me
can still see the

tall glasses that
seem summery on what
is the longest day

Soon the light

will go she says
the days get shorter.
I can't bear
she murmurs, *another*

winter in Stowe and
I think how different
this isolation is,
this iced tea, this

time that stretches
where little grows
as it did, green
as that mint, except

my mother, smaller,
more distant, gaunt

TAKING MY MOTHER TO THE BATHROOM

I lead her, a
child waking up
from a nightmare,
dazed by light.
She lags, hurries
then, half cranky,
half grateful.
She wants the
door shut, then
says open it,
wants my hands
the right way,
wash in between
my fingers. She
says the wash-
cloth is too
wet, too cold,
too soapy. The
towels are too
heavy. You don't
she spits, cover
your mouth. Go
home, you should
not be here to
see me like this

MY MOTHER AND THE LILACS

Their purple meant
spring. "That whole
apartment was
lilacs," she glows,
retelling how
the one she
couldn't marry
but checks for
in phone books
fifty years,
surprised her
with orchid
and snow. She
wishes for a yard,
for daughters
who will plant
lilacs that
bloom, not just
stunted twigs
shadowed by pine.
Unlike card games,
where the one
with nothing wins,
what never bloomed
haunts the most

CURLING ON THE BOTTOM OF MY MOTHER'S BED

as she would
on mine in
different houses,
bring me iced tea
at midnight or
cold chicken we'd
devour with our
fingers after
a date. I don't
think she minded
having to take
my arm in dark
restaurants
or crossing the
street, a good
reason to touch
me as she does
more freely now
as light in June
starts shriveling.
We whisper to
each other these
past 41 days we
haven't been apart,
like new lovers
who feel what
they have so rare
they can't bear
to sleep apart

THE LILACS MY MOTHER NEVER GOT

tho once her rooms were
filled with that orchid
musk. *To the ceiling*
she says. A surprise
from the man she
couldn't marry. Like
the house she never
had, she plans for lilacs,
clips articles on slip
covers, drapes, folds
them like soft flannel
for a child stillborn.
She sees outlines, the
front lawn daughters
won't be ashamed to
bring boys to in albums
she dates carefully as
if to prove real

LIKE SOME ANCIENT CHINESE

My mother wanted to take what
she cherished with her. No jade,
not the emerald she mostly saw
as flawed, no statues or photo-
graphs of her mother: she wanted
me to go with her. If she could
not phone to see how I got home
from a trip or the mall, she could

not rest. *"You're so thin,"* she
said over and over, *"we could be
buried in the same space."* Though
she liked living alone as long as
she could phone me, eternity with-
out AT&T seemed a scary way to
any long sleep. If I could be close,
as I was in the room already half

underground, like a pajama party,
or a college dorm she grinned
over pills and IV, it might not be
so bad she didn't get back to the
ocean and never got to Europe
or the west coast to lie back with
her mouth full of dirt and never tell
the stories and secrets she meant to

if she could still touch me

LOOKING FOR THE LOST VOICES

(other voices)

SLEEPING WITH LORCA

It's not true, he never chose women.
I ought to know. It was Grenada and
the sun falling behind the Alhambra was
flaming lava. I could say I was
too but some things should be left unsaid.
But I remember his fingers on the buttons
at the back of my neck, my skin burned
as he fumbled with rhinestones and pearls.
I want you breathed into my neck though
perhaps he was whispering *Green,
green I want you green.* How little he
needed to impress me with his poems.
One English term paper with them and I
was naked, taken. It wouldn't matter if
he had a potbelly or stank of garlic.
My jeans were a puddle around my
knees. I was the gored bull, hypnotized
by moves I'd only imagined but never
believed would enter me. There's
more you might coax me to say but
for now, it's enough I can still smell the
green wind, that 5 o'clock in the afternoon
that would never be another time

MY AFTERNOONS WITH DYLAN THOMAS

It was just a blur, like you might think,
stumbling from the White Horse Tavern,
the maples already tinged with blood.
He wasn't booming and loud, he wasn't
his voice, wasn't that poet booming
on records, all Swansea and raging.
There was no wild dying of the light.
We stopped for egg creams. He loved

them better than the cream of a woman's
thighs many say he collapsed in, took
the long-legged bait and shipwrecked,
but it was the cove of skin, the warmth,
everything unlike the dark coal mines or
the gray mist of Rhemmy. I won't forget
the softness of his curls. He wasn't my
type, too fair and he didn't work out,

his body soft as his lips. He was more
like a pet, a kitten I could let cuddle
against me. Was I a virgin? What does
that matter. Or whether he was a good
lover. When he held my cat, who
always hissed at new people, she let
him press her into his skin, as if, like
when he held me, her fur could keep

fear from spilling and staining the
rest of Wednesday

ROSE DEVORAH

dreams of old houses
in Russia, licorice hair
fire licks as lace is
scorched, turns ash
before the wedding
and the bride's bones
are dust in the
rose light green
is sucked from as sun
sets in the after-
noon. Some unknown
aunt she could have
been named for maybe,
wild, intense as rare
tea roses or Rashmi
Rose incense burnt in
a room the walls
pulled from floats
thru frames that are
like mirrors, her
raw cheeks like
cherries in the rain
or blood from a wild
deer running, turning
snow color of plums

ALBERTA HUNTER

long gold hoops flashing,
eyes flashing, hands
on her hips. Nothing
on her isn't moving.
"gonna lay it on
you." Born in
Memphis. *"Got a*
nickel for bread. Put
it on the sidewalk,
went to Chicago.
Never knew my kisses
meant so much, never
dreamed life had so."
She's 85, laying it
on you, dancing,
belting it,
her hair pulled
straight back not
to miss anything

GEORGIA O'KEEFFE

I can see shapes

it's as if my mind
created shapes

some repeat themselves

sand pink tops
a mountain
sun, bleached skull
of deer

a black iris
I wanted the black
to make you feel
what I was
feeling

your eye pulled to its center

      ***

I painted my first skull

from a barrel of bones

the cow's head
against the blue

I like the shapes,
they have no-

thing to do with death

181

mountains thru the
holes in a bone

bones against the sky
bones and moons
bones and flowers
a reddish bone with a yellow sky

        ***

I put up all my paintings
and saw how in each
one I'd tried to
please someone

took them down

put them away

there were things I
wanted to say

I sat on the floor
worked against the
closet door

        ***

her hair bound
on top of her head

"the first year here
because there weren't any
flowers I began

picking up bones"
a whole pile in the patio

bones like flowers

her hair the color of
bones, of the lightest lilacs

      ***

I loved Texas
light coming on the plains

huge dust storms

sometimes I'd come in I couldn't
tell it was me
except for my shape

I'd be the color of the road

EARLY SUNDAY MORNING

Edward Hopper

The thing about Sunday is
the light moving across
a two-story red brick
building, shops on the
first floors, four dark
doorways and a barber
pole. The shops are closed.
They'll stay closed all
day. 1930. Sunday floating
in space, beating out
Saturday for quiet. It's
an old neighborhood that
has known better days. You
never ask what day it is.
Sunday feels like Sunday.
A Sunday kind of love,
never on Sunday. When Emily
Dickinson wrote "there's
a certain slant of light
that oppresses…" it must
have been Sunday, a day like
wide water without a sound

MOONRISE, HERNANDEZ, NEW MEXICO 1941

Ansel Adams

past adobe, deep behind tumbleweed
someone shuts off a radio, as if news
of war would come over the sage, slither thru
dust and locusts. Under a pale moon
crosses gleam. In streaked light

a young girl unbuttons a hand-me-down
blouse, lets it fall to the linoleum,
thinks of her brother crawling on his belly
in the South Pacific. Her breasts swell, her
hair smells of pinyon and agave.

She hears her father playing banjo on the front porch,
thinks of her mother's leathery skin, lank hair,
swears it won't always be like this: nights with
nothing but the wind in the mesquite,
vows to escape, make it to a place where there is more
than sky and mountains, where women dress in high heels
and smell of roses like in movie magazines

maybe get all the way to
Albuquerque

THE WOMAN IN LOVE WITH MAPS

aches for the old
ones, dusky as an
abandoned ghost town
where the wooden
pier is driftwood.
She doesn't want
longitudes and
latitudes, favors
roads mutable as
a bracelet made
of sand she can
write an SOS on to
the wind. She dreams
of islands, magical
as the fingers of
the concert pianist,
each with its own
intelligence and
breath. She wants
the light to be what
photographers long
for, the magic hour
flecked with the color
of violet dusk, the
names of cities
exotic as spices or
words in another
language: *empanadas,
estrellita, la trisleza.*
Or the words left on
a Persian jar of lilies,
Dear Heart and then,
the way there

THE WOMAN WHO LOVED MAPS

Not for accuracy, she is tired of facts and distance,
longitude, unless it's carved out in aquamarine
and violet. She doesn't want carefully engineered, exact
miles, doesn't want to leave the draped rooms the old

parchment and linens are spread out in, throws out her
AAA map, her Frommer's, her Michelin, doesn't want the
careful blotches, the interstates, but loves those old
picture maps where flying monsters with lavender wings
inhabit islands mysterious as Rorschachs or hieroglyphs
almost too devastating to read, wants what shimmers and
intoxicates like velvets and old Persian rugs. It's too
exhausting to pack and unpack, she doesn't want to find her-

self stranded in Istanbul or Tangiers in the rain and
no taxi. It's easier, she tells herself, to love maps than
men who'll roll away from the pillow, whispering "for her
own good," or: "it wasn't you, it was me." She wants to run

her fingers over their pale tourmaline and rusts, old as
teapots from Persia, the oldest Venetian glass. She doesn't
want exact latitudes, but what is mysterious as a room behind
drawn lace, lips she won't have to do laundry for. She aches for a

country in the shape of a fly-blue fish washed with lemon,
something she can date with one glance, something from
the fifteenth century. Not what folds up, can split along
the crease, wants what she can lie smooth in a locked flat drawer

or roll up to have there in the dark just for her

AUGUST 18, 1587

Virginia Dare, first English child born in the new country. Her grandfather went back to England to get help, came back 3 years later but there was no sign of any of them

In that fall, as leaves went
blood with her child squalling
her mother must have clawed
wisteria, dreamt of orange trees
loaded with fruit as ice crept
into buckets and the dark came
too fast. No one knows if the
corn faltered, the flood bank
rose. No one knows if a roof
collapsed, bones broke, if men
crept in with hatchets, the baby
in her arms as snow piled higher
than the chinked window. The
mother might have torn the dress
she wore for teas in Essex into
swaths to soothe her child's
burning skin, or to make a doll's
dress for the corncob figure her
child giggled and cried to have
near her bed. Were there gaps
in her memory, going over the
smell of English roses, the weather,
the porcelain cups for tea. She
could load the gun but would
she use it on a stranger in the
middle of the night with the baby
between them? Did she hold it in
her hands as if it was another's
fingers as the moon slithered thru
burlap and the rough weave never
let her forget where she was

THE ICE MAIDEN'S 232nd SOS

Peru's Ampato Ice Maiden is the first frozen Incan female mummy, and her body may be the best-preserved of any found in the Americas from pre-Colombian times. Believed to be 500 years old, the mummy was discovered near the summit of 20,700-foot Mount Ampato in the Peruvian Andeas. A girl of about 12–13 years of age, she was probably offered as a sacrifice by Incan priests.

You wouldn't think that,
buried so long,
I could even respond again.
That I could hear sleet,
the branches over me
creaking and splintering.
Sometimes, I imagine
sun and light leaking through stone
that was a dream.
Then it was over.
I can't tell you how
I left what was my world for so long,
and that the first glimpse of sky
seemed like water,
my body like a pleated skirt
pressed under granite,
dark as violets,
rigid as bark,
terrified as I fell through ice crystals,
still as ice crystals,
seeing flesh and fingers
before I could feel them

THE ICE MAIDEN'S 267th SOS

I'm a teenager,
true,
but I've been one
for 500 years,
and the further I get
from the last day,
the more I see my mother
more clearly.
How really,
there was nothing that she could do
as a woman to save me.
The weak always lie,
too terrified to say what's true.
She gave her dearest gift,
was left with nothing.
Maybe she thought it was a test,
asked to sacrifice
a daughter like Abraham and Isaac.
I thought that I might find her
under the earth,
another myth.
Don't call me Persephone.
There was no Demeter,
no Zeus.

No nothing.

Whatever I hoped,
I never found in that garden.
I was as foolish as someone
who believes that something
will grow from planting a
dead child in the ground

WANT HAIR—THE ICE MAIDEN'S BLUES

It begs for your fingers,
even through glass.
Don't lean too close,
the sign says, as if the iced mummy
could contaminate you,
while it's the other way around.
Once I had eggshell skin
that they sacrificed even before
I needed what you now call a Tampax.
In my village,
we braided cocoa leaves
between our thighs,
or we were called the red-legged women.
Red's always been a favorite color in my town.
See how it glistens
through the weave of my wrap.
I've want hair,
people still murmur.
I read lips through
the fog of my refrigerated case.
It's what I most was,
what I most wanted to fill
with night's jasmine, and the sounds of Java birds.
My hair never frizzed in the jungle,
or dried out at Cuzco.
Sometimes I dream it's my mother's hair,
unbound,
as she never was,
flowing and free,
revolutionary as it would have been
for her to save me.
You can see your own face
in the shine of my onyx locks.
I used to wonder if the man

who smashed my head into the rocks
first saw his eyes in that black mirror,
if he could smell the apricots
I washed it with,
if, like a body falling into the river,
his own face crumbled with mine

JEANNE MARIE PLOUFFE

(after reading Carolyn Forché)

Small and dark behind your mother's full skirts
as she cleaned other people's houses.
Florence and I imagined worms slithered thru you
when you ate lumps of sugar in my grandmother's
bathroom, still stayed thin. Eyes like cloves

under huge lashes in classes you wouldn't say
a word in. *Canuck* the boys called out
over Otter Creek Bridge as your legs got less
spindly and the girls from college professors'
homes didn't invite you. People said your last name

with the tone they'd say tramp. Your skin creamy,
your hair curled with night. There wasn't a boy
who didn't think he could put his hand inside
your dress. You never said anything,
as if a part of you was already gone,

as if there was some place to go. Once,
singing of Quebec, your eyes gleamed like the gold
cross boys yanked from your neck and tossed in the snow.
I hear the trailer burned down, the survivors
headed north. Jeanne Marie, if you read this

please write me

SHE WAITS LIKE SOME SHARP CHEDDAR IN THE PANTRY

huddling in the dark
on the shelf
less exotic
maybe than
women flashy as
Camembert,
intense as St. André's
soft cheese,
less outgoing
and sure of their
direction than
women who know
who they are,
like Jarlsberg or
Swiss, clean-cut,
in suits, sipping
Chardonnay as
leaves go blood
and burnt sienna.
She prides
herself on being
free of holes a
tongue or finger
could get stuck
in. Only her
thighs soften,
so long alone,
still creamy as
Havarti, as blue
spreads under wraps
where what ripens
is dying

THE WOMAN WHO LOVED MAPS

lusts for the old ones,
no AAA maps with their
crisp trail of exits
and entrances, no
Michelin guides with

blotched hotels, what
you should see. She
lusts for maps with
tinctures no one still
knows how to make,

madders of roses that
don't still grow,
a wash of lime, myrrh,
abalone. She's a woman
who's been around,

she's had her cravings
and now its for maps.
She can plunge into the
mysterious shapes of
islands that didn't

exist, more lush, more
tempting. She wants to
spread the maps above
her on her bed like
lovers she can taste,

let lure, and then lock
back in drawers there
is only her key for

THIS DECEMBER

A swan moved into the house, camouflaged
among geese. She must have been, or the
mist from the pond blurred her. I say *her*
because her antics never seemed male. Never
threatening, but coy. And never loitering
on my side of the bed. I suppose she was
cold or starved. This year, the pond froze
early. When I think back, I remember a white
feather on the deck but that wasn't so strange.
The tangerines were gnawed before they were
ripe. It could have been crows or gulls I
told myself after the space between my lover
and me in bed got wider. He thought this
whiteness was lovely as he had psychotic
ballet dancer lovers who became swans. The
quilt's full of feathers he'd insist when a
pale wreathe of her circled the sheets. I thought
it was more like something wild staking territory.
It wasn't that we really saw her though it is
clear the cat did. She was more of a presence
and haunting as a dead love whose handwriting
lures and chills. I felt her watch him. She
knew his moods, each move and had more time to
plot seduction than I did. Being unattainable
didn't hurt. He felt her breath and his blood
couldn't sleep. Drugs hardly helped but for
once, he didn't mind not sleeping. When he turned
up music too loud for me, she moved into his arms
downstairs. I kept typing. I could feel her legs
sprawled open like a dancer with a miracle 180-degree
arabesque, hardly human, a wild open grin. Crumbs
and bread disappeared. There were more feathers,
it was like a mist and the moon was hazy through her
as if a storm was coming. Once when I opened an old

quilt from Odessa the room filled with its snow.
Some days seemed as opaque. The day the pond froze
for good the house felt somehow different. The cat
stopped being spooked. A downstairs window looked
splintered but then I saw it was only frost etched
in what looked like a hieroglyph, something in a
language I don't know. I vacuumed up the last
feathers. The stain of wings still hangs in the
air, gives the room a bluish light. Still, her
leaving wasn't like a breakup where someone leaves
the house, packs a painting, favorite gloves but
more the way something comes apart, as it did, so
slowly it's hard to tell when what isn't wasn't
still whole

EVEN BEFORE THE POND FROZE

there were traces, even before blood
leaves fell from the oak, the feathers
began to move closer. There were always
some in the grass the mallards and wild
geese grazed in. But these were totally

white, smelling vaguely of roses. First
I thought the scent was my own skin. Or the
tea roses in the garden. But something wilder
mixed in. I could feel a shadow, even in the
brightest light, something like me but not

me. Sometimes in the mirror, I feel her pale
eyes right behind me like a daughter I never
chose. If I knew Morse code, maybe I'd have
understood the tapping on glass at night. One
morning an envelope with no postage appeared on

the stairs and handwriting I had to put up
to the mirror to read said, "Leda's daughter,"
and I thought of the feathers rising up
thicker, piling against lawn chairs on the deck
until the sun goes. I think of a woman raped

by a swan, her face white as lilies. Some-
thing dissolving the way men melted, snow on
the battlefields in Fredericksburg. The
flutter of wings and claws become shadows,
the deepest black. Even now, this long later,

it flutters over the grass, wild to
soar above earth her mother was ground into,
to use the wings that used her, soar above
everything she's heard the stories of to
redefine *ravishing*

THE MAD GIRL TAKES THE RADIO OUT OF THE ROOM

takes the batteries
out of it, cuts
the electric cord
to not be haunted
by the talk jock
she'd lured with
cryptic notes
when she still
could write, verbs
sharp, luscious
as he said her
lips were after
noons as the blue
spread of roses
went from red to
flesh where she
laughed, threatened
to keep him pinned
leaning against
the nightstand like
a totem, plastic
as his glib gaff, an
air hostage in
lilac light until
leaving, he says
thanks and suddenly
the xxx's on the
shower door no
longer stand
for kisses

THE MAD GIRL HUMS "I GOT ALONG WITHOUT YOU BEFORE I MET YOU"

down Union Street in
warm mist, knows
when you write some-
thing it often
becomes true later.
Cocoa eyes stare
back in the mirror,
for once, not the
color of red lilacs
that still haven't
bloomed. She thinks
how when she
scrawled "more" it
looked like "none,"
of those blue sheet
May nights, remote
as fishing villages
past Stockholm,
how if you stare
at the sun too long
it can take
days of darkness
to see again. And
even then, there
are ghosts

BARBIE HUNTS THRU MEDICAL BOOKS LOOKING FOR WHAT IS WRONG WITH HER WHEN SHE SEES HER BIRTH DATE IN A BOOK, KNOWS SHE IS OVER 30

and feels so
hollow inside,
unfulfilled,
as if all she's
done is change
her clothes.
She wonders a-
bout the women's
movement, maybe
she frowns it's
the change and
she hasn't even
had a baby, had a
period, a
hair that was
not in place.
Perfection that
can be shelved,
one yank and I'd
be bald, naked.
She flips thru
chapters on
neurosis, wonders
if it's hormones
she lacks. Where
she's been, hardly
seems to matter:
the beach, Sun
Valley, Spain.
It's all façade,

going thru the
motions. What
did a wedding
get me she groans
I never was free-
moving, as they
said in 1975
but empty, full
of holes—some-
thing just for
someone else
to collect or abuse

NAVY BARBIE

wants to see the world,
she does get a little
seasick but likes
the white uniform, tho
the skirt is a little
too loose and long for
her taste. Still it might
be a change she can go
with. Actually, the sequins
dug into her shoulders,
the ballerina tulle
scratched, and tho it was
kept secret, fun fur
made her sneeze. And
forget the Parisian
Bonjour look: that was
the worst, a cameo
choker size of a plum
or a small coconut
wedged against her larynx,
so she says "when I tried
to say yes or no it
scraped, and the lace
under my arms—talk
about sandpaper. But
the worst was those fish-
net hose, rough, and the
garter, Jesus, grating,
my toes burned from that
pattern, crammed into
high-heeled platform
open toes and the hair-
piece with feathers. At
least in the Navy they've

actually," she smiles,
"given me something to
read. My hair is natural.
I'm authentic. First
Class Petty Officer.
I finally am more than
just a pretty. I rank"

BARBIE WONDERS ABOUT BUYING A COFFIN

if she'll need one,
not that these
plastic boxes she's
in so long on a
shelf aren't like
being buried in a
toy box under eaves,
freezing in winter,
scorched by June.
She wonders if they
will bury her in a
ballerina costume,
a rodeo suit, if
they'll shave her
hair or braid it.
Just because she's
empty doesn't mean
she doesn't care. Or
that her velvet or
tulle, even her under-
pants have been stripped
from her and she was
left nude as some
one in the camps
about to march into
gas, doesn't mean
she doesn't want
to know if she'll
go with one of her
many scarves around
her, à la Isadora.
Or if Ken, supposing

she's eyeing a Ricky
or P.T. or Alan,
even trying Christy,
rages in, beans her
with his boogie board,
strangles her with
the ropes of his
Hawaiian fun hammock
or poisons her with
cyanide in soda
from the All American
store, runs her over
in a remote control
Corvette and leaves
her in the trunk
with nothing to wear
for this last stop

MARILYN MONROE POSES ON RED SATIN

I

never supposes
when she could
have been past
60 someone will
pay more than
she's ever earned
for the pout of
her lips, the
way blood color
reflects onto
her nipples.
She's cold and
wishes there was
a different way
to make a buck,
but at least it
is acting, pre-
tending, spread
eagle, a bore.
No, nightmare.
The satin feels
like the inside
of a mouth. She
could be a sliver
of melon sliding
thru, knowing
there is only
one way she
will get out

II

she's heard it
will make her
tits more red,
leans back
tries to imagine
this, isn't
happy, like some-
one under someone
they'd never choose
who is pumping
away. She hears
a train whistle,
quietly hums a
few leaving blues,
has to pee but
doesn't. The
slick cloth is
cold as a strange
tongue wedged
deep inside her.
Blue would have
been more her,
but "red," the
photographer
whistled, "would
touch men's
blood, make them
want to charge."

JESUS AND MADONNA

He was writing poems about her when I first met him.
It wasn't only her fame—to him she was a lost
sheep, a lost sweet and he always said there but
for the grace of. He was thinking how his mother
was a madonna too and who was he to judge her.

Actually, I think he found her sexy and he
always wanted to multiply and be fruitful. And even
in those days, Madonna was talking about wanting to
have a child, wanting the perfect father. To come
out of one madonna and enter into another would

be a miracle I suppose. I guess I was a little
jealous. I tried to convince myself he was
attracted to her because he wanted to save her
and there was a lot to save her from. I know
someone said, maybe in *People* magazine, that

when J.C. cured a blind man, let him, after years
of darkness, see the light again, he didn't want
anyone to know he did these miracles but somehow
it got out. I think he planned this. In fact, it
was probably Madonna's fame that got him going after

years of being all over the world in his mother's arms
on stamps as the baby Jesus, now, handsome and strong—
all the women said it, and smelling so nice too, a stamp
where he's in the arms of another madonna might bring
out the *National Enquirer,* rekindle the fervor of those

early days. Even *Nightline* and CNN would spread his word,
in English and 52 languages and Leno and Letterman would
fall prostrate before him, kissing his feet on the air

YEARS LATER LORENA THINKS OF THE PENIS SHE HAD FOR A DAY

how, in her hand,
it was so much
less angry,
more like a
scared bird,
not the weapon
she'd known
but shriveling,
scared, a wounded
kitten coiled
into itself, into
her hands as if
she was skin, a
caul it could
find refuge in.
It was no
longer a fist
of blood, punching,
a sword of bone
and because it
seemed to
quiver, dream of
flight she'd
just let it go

CONDOM CHAIN LETTER

use this condom
and then send it on
to the name at the
bottom. You will
be rewarded in
15 days with 11
used safes. Do not
discard. One man did
not believe in this and
a wasp the size of
New England invaded
his house. Now he won't
need more. Your luck
will change soon.
20 condoms won't be
enough for one night:
women will flock to
you as if the tips
were coded with
something they've
felt and need
again. You can't
lose. Put this down
and let your dog eat
it—one man did
and his penis withered
to a thimble of dusty
skin, a feather
crows swooped down
to use for their nest.
That was the last
he saw of it. Send 75
used condoms. Your
hemorrhoids will

disappear. Only your
wallet and your
penis will get bigger.
Another man who threw
this chain letter away lost
everything that extended
more than half an inch
from his body to sharks.
And when he finally
sent it on, fingers and
thighs grew back, his
nose and ear, even a
nub of a penis.
This is no joke

IN THE DARKNESS OF NIGHT

(war poems)

WAR

the woman is
amazed not
that the watch
store is
open but that
anyone cares
about the time,
or knows it.
Every part of
her an aide, a
scout sent
out to listen,
to bring back
news to empty
rooms where
people who
hoped it would
be over are
no longer

I REMEMBER HAIFA BEING LOVELY BUT

there were snakes in the
tent. My mother was
strong but she never
slept, was afraid of
dreaming. In Auschwitz
there was a numbness,
lull of just staying
alive. Her two babies
gassed before her, Dr.
Mengele, you know who
he is? She kept her
young sister alive
only to have her die
in her arms the night
of liberation. My mother
is big-boned, but she
weighed under 70 lbs.
It was hot, I thought
the snakes lovely. No
drugs in Israel, no
food. I got pneumonia,
my mother knocked the
doctor to the floor
when they refused,
said I lost two in
the camp and if this
one dies I'll kill
myself in front of
you. I thought that
once you became a
mother, blue numbers
appeared, mysteriously,
tattooed on your arm

SHE SAID THE GEESE

When she saw them
squabbling over a
crust she started
shivering. But in
the light she felt
the shadows, how
on their knees, in
the camps the young
and old battered wildly
in mud for the dry
bread. A mouthful
thrown for hundreds,
the smallest,
the frail trampled.
She said the corn
slid thru her
hands. She couldn't
move, toss a crumb.
They weren't geese,
only men and women,
someone dressed in her
sister's clothes,
clawing and scratching
blood and dust

BLACK RAIN, HIROSHIMA

It was as if we
were thrown into
a smelting furnace.
My friend had skin
hanging down like
the meltings of a
candle. Many ran
to the cool of any
water they could
find, hurled them
selves into sewers
or headed for the
River Ota that
soon was thick with
the dead and dying.
Some died on the
riverbank, their
heads in the water
having used their
last surge of earthly
energy for a drink

*

Hiromu Morishiti found
her father later that
day lying in a grassy
field. He'd been on
a street car near
downtown, on his
way to work. She
cremated him in
her garden that
night, his eyes
like those grilled
fish. Others slept on
Hijiama Hill, looked
down on the place that
once was their city,
lay calling for
mothers, calling
for children, calling
for water then not
calling at all

IN THE VA HOSPITAL

You wouldn't believe
the jokes, we were
all glad to get
there and not in
body bags, at least we
could sing and ogle
blondes, those of us
with eyes still and
lips that could move.
I'd have been out
sooner than 12 months
if it wasn't for the
skin grafts. No one
felt funny because
nobody had everything
they'd been born with.
Even the quadriplegics
would go on about girls.
Even in the copters
with blood filling the
cockpit, matting
hair, the first thing
those who could talk
whimpered or moaned
was, "Hey, mate, do I
still have my balls?"

SEEING THE DOCUMENTARY OF THE LIBERATION OF BERGEN-BELSEN

The bodies like driftwood
tangling, naked. Pale
as marble or roots of
trees suddenly torn
from the earth that
held it like the
scalped shrunken head
of the Polish scientist
who tried to run,
unreal as the man
shot when he chewed
earth to get out of
the cell for air, the
bottom half of his body
burning. Bodies stacked
like wood, a cross
dangling, child frozen
into a breast, his
legs cut off, wrinkled
little hot dogs

I GOT THE BUCKS FIGURE A LONG SLOW

summer van ride up
through Canada, soak up
the cool green and then
I got to go, keep
on. I can't just stay
in this room here. I'll
never work for any-
body. After 'Nam
I tried the dream,
the white-picket
handcuffs, married
her out of pity,
ass-kissed the
school. No more—you
think I've been offensive? You
ain't seen—watch out for my dog,
he's mean and it's not show.
I want to get them
for what they
turned me into. I got Librium,
vodka, a machete in the
top drawer. Machine gun
I polish, check each
night. Got medals in
a velvet zip bag
thrown into the corner.
In the photographs
near the mattress on
the floor, I'm 22,
trim, got a Vietnamese
girl with long hair
dripping spread eagle
on each knee. And these
were the dogs. They

couldn't remove
the shrapnel, too close
to the spine. You see the
way my body's shaking?
I'll take some books
on 'Nam, on the Holocaust.
Yeah, get me a van, pack up
my mean, old dog and
slide down the west
coast. Gotta figure
how to get guns over the border. Did
you know I spoke Spanish
my first 4 years? Gonna
get me to El Salvador.
You know whose
side *I'll* be on

LIKE THAT

the men toppling over
shot in the back
It was as if their
heads were too heavy

the difference between who
got it and didn't,
as accidental as typing
treat instead of threat

IT WAS LIKE WINTERGREEN

a camouflage
over the babies'
graves. Even as
the Americans
marched in, 2000
were killed. While
the Germans were
surrendering, they
put ivy over the
earth where arms
and legs were
still sticking up.
The Americans
made them rebury
the dead. But the
Germans didn't
put flowers or
memorials over
the prisoners of
war, just left
wintergreen. It
doesn't need light,
it doesn't need
care. You don't have
to think about it

THERE WERE ALWAYS STARS

at night, loud,
exploding the
closeness of
wrinkled silk.
I remember the
smell of my
mother's hair
holding me
curled into her
coolness of
marble and the
hard lines
of a chair
shading us, the
wood becoming
a tree again.
Blue of sky.
Trees in the
bottom of a
teacup. Even
when the one
wall was ash
mother scrubbed
and kept lace
squares on half
the couch, lit
candles. One Friday
bed posts flared
wilder than wax in
silver. It was
all we knew, blue-
berry jam blue
veins breaking, the
blue of violets,

Nana's blue sweater
one arm shorter,
unraveling...
Shapes dissolve
like margarine
high noon on the
Sahara. Blue the last
color. David's eyes as
the train door shut.
Blue tattoo, blue
flame I'd only
touch once. Every-
thing transformed the
way a scalp stuns,
shaved of hair

TREBLINKA

like the sound
of giraffe
necks shattering,
trembling.
Crystal bullets.
I was wrapped
in a blue so
torn and old
it was almost
colorless, blue
of David's eyes
and the light
we could see from
trains. I had
enough of moon-
light, hiding,
crawling between
barns. Under the
hay my heart was
pounding. Maybe
when they shave
my hair it will
go for a mattress
in Berlin, for
that man I'd
love to spit
at who dreams
of goose fat
sputtering as
he washes his
coarse beard
with soap made
of a sister
you won't know.

If Treblinka was
a color it would
be a hard icy
almost white
blue the color
of flames
they shoved
cribs into. What
shatters becomes
its own blade

SHE SAID I KNOW IT'S ALMOST MIDNIGHT BUT I WANTED TO GIVE YOU THE BARE SKELETON

My father was rich, a Czech. First it was
just the Gypsies. Nobody worried but then
they started liquidating businesses. Mother
looked rich. Jews started having to carry
papers. On a train she saw these young boys
pulling an old man's beard, jabbing his
yamulke. My mother hissed *isn't this
action beneath you?* No one thought she
was a Jew. When they left, she, who mostly
spoke pure German, tried to use the little
Yiddish she knew, but the man on the train
backed away. She was a rough cookie. Had
her kids yanked by Mengele, mother beaten.
Once she had to kneel in a snowbank in a
dress of small, pale, faded blue flowers.
She came to days later, lived to keep her
sister alive. Each morning friends walked
to the wet ground near the tall electrified
fence, curled near it, couldn't take it.
My mother got them all to turn around, said
she knew they would get out. I was born in
1945 in a tent in Israel, wrapped in a torn
blanket. My mother who never washed a diaper,
never had seen a cow up close turned them
to pets, got pails of milk from one they let
sleep near the bed. At night I heard her
whisper about the camps, how her sister died
the night of liberation in her arms, gasped
it's getting dark then she was gone. Mama said
if she'd known what would happen, she would
not have let her suffer so long. There were

230

roaches in the tent, no food but I didn't know
we were poor. I just thought it was the way
it was, the way once you became a mother, with
breasts and hair down there, blue numbers also
appeared as mysteriously on your skin

YOU TAKE FOR GRANTED

the dripping lilacs, blue petals
battered, holding on, holding
their brightness in hot, steamy
air as if to become brighter
once hail melts from the

slick, dark stems. A postcard wouldn't
do it. How much should I try to
tell you? If there was a
photograph I'd be the blonde
in the black velvet
fitted suit. It would be Cape
Anne in November. The lilacs would
have flamed and pulled away,

a summer romance
now short as the weeks. The
woman, let's think of her as
a spy, maybe, guerilla, stealing
into where no one else
could go, camouflaged
as some poet, man-crazed, a

little flaky who visits
rooms she can't stay in,
undresses and lies down with

danger, cocky enough to suppose
she couldn't lose her skin
or her balance. The blue
of lilacs, her
veins thru flesh cashmere,
roadmaps to places where
there are road blocks.

Even if I was alive,
scars would have
been worn from what
tied me. You take the
lilacs for granted,
the blue leaves in the
bottom of Dresden china,
cyanide glowing with
a blue light that
zaps like no lover

WHO HELD THE CAMERA SO STEADILY, AND WHY?

Photographs
at the Holocaust Museum:
In black and white
a naked girl,
maybe six,
gripped by the neck
in the hands of a woman
with huge biceps.
*A mentally disturbed girl
shortly before her murder.*
Near the dangling girl
is a photo in summer—
trees are fully leafed,
dark smoke pours
out of one building.
Down the hall
a young woman with glasses
takes aim at a man
kneeling
in front of a pit of bodies:
the pistol points at the neck
so no shattered bone
will fly his way

HE'S MOVED EVERYTHING HE NEEDS
INTO ONE ROOM

walls of books on
the Holocaust, revolutions,
Iraq and 'Nam block
the light. Paper from
D-Day, divorce
papers with stains of cups
all over. The velvet
zip bag of medals, part
of the moat around the
mattress he's
curled on under
a brushed cotton quilt:
you couldn't call any-
thing in this room
a comforter. Crumbs
from the last three
weeks, machete
in a top drawer, machine
guns, a .44, Librium
crumbled near ashes,
punching bag, the
insides spill out
like *entrails*
in the jungle he said
I took the man's
intestines, washed them
off in rainwater,
stuffed them back into
the slit like
squeezing bread
crumbs into a turkey

HEARING OF REAGAN'S TRIP TO BITBURG

as new leaves turn
the size of babies'
hands, the last
thing mothers saw
as the screaming,
wriggling bodies were
thrown in fires, hands
buried above some grave
as if waving goodbye
or pulling you with
them. Suddenly I'm
back in the yellow
room, color of daffodils
breaking down. Woke
up each night dreaming
of tunnels and fire,
the words whispered in
front of the apartment,
rain of the blue
tattoos. The gas,
words like *cattle car*
changed as the word
camp, so when I went
to Camp Hochelaga I
waited for gas, held
my breath, couldn't
sleep with lights off

IF HAIR COULD SIFT DOWN

make a silt soft as the
three feet of rose petals
Cleopatra had surrounding
her bed, a swamp for lovers to

open in or a lake of soft
rose leaves, the sheets on the bed
would float in the musk waves.
Hair shaved, leaving the women in line

whimpering. *For cleanliness is*
next to signs said. Nobody
didn't want to believe though
the air was strange smoke.

If braids chopped from a young girl
days before she'll even bleed, herded
over stone, her mother singing
Hatikvah could drift back, hang

on trees like Spanish moss
or float onto a snow field out
from mattresses and pillows they
were shoved into for years in a

Gestapo son's wife's closet,
if they could yank free as the
skull it once hugged couldn't,
except in a last breath in fire,

a bird might pluck what didn't go
cinders, what escaped in a
rough officer's hand before the head
was left in the square on a stick

for warning, an eye sliding down
to mud. Fifty years later, what
cushioned the lips pressing a young girl
in an attic they hid and warmed,

brushed 200 times by the light of a candle
might be woven into a nest in dark
pines, make a cove feathers would
uncoil in, fragile and wild to fly

as what the hair once held

GALE OF THE SUN, THE ANGELS DON'T FLY

(place)

NORTH OF COTTONWOOD

rose lichen
　　gamble oak
　　　globe mallow

bent in rain

blue lupine

juniper mistletoe

it rains and keeps raining

these rocks
　　　pulled from each other

two million years ago

wrenched like a woman
whose child is grabbed

on a cattle car

smashed into stone

her eyes, streaked
　　like tonight's sky

a Monday, all *sipapu,*

a spirit entrance

into the underworld

ARIZONA RUINS

Past Mogollon River
        the limestone ruins
scrape it with your finger
                and the floor breaks

                        The talc
                must have dusted
        their dark
bodies as they squatted on these
        floors grinding
mesquite and creosote

No one knows
        where they went
                from the cliffs
        with their
                earth jars and sandals

Or if they
cursed the
        desert moon
                as they wrapped
their dead
        babies
                in bright cloth
                        and jewels

242

2

Now cliff swallows
    nest in the mud
        where the Sinagua
    lived
        until water ran out

High in these white cliffs
    weaving yucca and cotton
        How many nights did they listen
    for cougar
        as they pressed the wet
            rust clay
        into bowls
    they walked
200 miles to trade in Phoenix
    before it was time to leave

40 years
before Columbus

3

Noon in the
caves

      it is summer the
            children are sleeping

The women
      listen to a story
      one of them has heard
      of an ocean

            Deer flesh dries in the sun
      they braid
willow stems
      and don't look up

When she
is done
      they are all
stoned on what could come
            from such water

It is cool and dark
      inside here

            This was the place

4

The others
have gone to find
salt and red
      stones for earrings

        The children

climb down

        To look for lizards
    and nuts he

    takes the girl he
wants
    for the first time

        Her blood cakes
           on the white chalk
floor

      Her thighs

        will make a bracelet
          in his head

5

Desert bees
    fall thru the wind
        over the pueblos
            velvet ash and barberry

They still find

        bodies
    buried in the wall
        a child's bones
      wrapped in yucca leaves
        and cotton

bats fly thru the
    ruins now
        scrape the charred
    walls white

        The people left
      the debris of their lives here
  arrows, dung
        And were buried
    with the bright
  turquoise they loved
      sometimes carved
  into animals and birds

CHAMPLAIN, BRANBURY, THE LAKES AT NIGHT

always women in the
dark on porches talking
as if in blackness their
secrets would be safe.
Cigarettes glowed like
Indian paintbrush.
Water slapped the
deck. Night flowers
full of things with wings,
something you almost
feel like the fingers
of a boy moving, as if
by accident, under
sheer nylon and felt
in the dark movie house
as the chase gets louder,
there and not there,
something miscarried
that maybe never was.
The mothers whispered
about a knife, blood.
Then, they were laughing
the way you sail out of
a dark movie theater
into wild light as if no-
thing that happened
happened

NEW HAMPSHIRE

wild cat in the
woodpile, deer

you can't see.
I drift with

the poem you
sent into an

underground
river where

Indians eat
fish so old

they have no
eyes. If I

shut my eyes
I hear the

water that
flows under

the columbine.
When I touch

the chair I hear
bluebirds that

were wild in its
leaves when there

were red flowers
in its branches

MIDDLEBURY POEM

Milky summer nights,
the men stay waiting, First National Corner
where the traffic light used to be, wait

as they have all June evenings of their lives.
Lilac moss and lily of the valley
sprout in the cooling air as

Miss Damon, never later for thirty years,
hurries to unlock the library, still
hoping for a sudden man to spring tall from the

locked dark of mysterious card catalogues to
come brightening her long dusty shelves.
And halfway to dark

boys with vacation bicycles
whistle flat stones over the bridge,
longing for secret places where
rocks are blossoming girls with damp thighs.

Then nine o'clock falls thick on lonely books
and all the unclaimed fingers and
as men move home through blue-metal light,
the Congregational Church bells

ringing as always four minutes late,
the first hayload of summer rumbles through
town and all the people shut their eyes
dreaming a wish

THIRTY MILES WEST OF CHICAGO

paint chips slowly.
It's so still you
can almost hear it
pull from a porch.

Cold grass claws
like fingers in a
wolf moon. A man
stands in corn bristles

listening, watching
as if something
could grow from
putting a dead child

in the ground

THINGS THAT SHINE IN QUEBEC CITY AS THE SUN FALLS

light on the ball
of glass, on
the puddles
under the Hilton.
The St. Lawrence glows,
the flag poles,
edges of buildings.
A yellow car in the
salmon light.
Lights are starting to go on.
Green copper roofs glow,
shadows of clouds
over sailboats
on the water.
The smell of leaves,
cool wind blowing.
The water
a ripple of light
like a flag of glass.
Diamond ripples.
I think of Diamond Head,
light that seemed
magical in a strange
town. The only
familiar sign is
one that says
Kresge's. Light
that will glow
when what
seems to
might not.
Green diamonds,
red diamonds,
blue diamonds
starting to cover
the hill

MIDWEST

all that sky
a flat black
with only a cat's
eyes blazing

people wait alone.
Wind changes in
the corn leaves.
People hear it like

a chord augmented.
Houses chip slowly
stranded in snow.
Only the sky is fast

MONET'S *LES NYMPHEAS*

the long curved
room, the walls

starting to
shimmer, breathe

A Chinese girl
sitting on the stone
bench next to me,

dazed, smiling

The lilies moving
into both of us

VIOLET JELLY

picking the leaves
Monday early in
a cool rain huddled
in wet sweatshirts.
Hours in the grey,
knees and fingers
numb. Our skin
smells of violets
while they soak
in the red pan
overnight till we
boil the green.
Then the pectin
turns them lilac.
We pour them into
glass, amethyst
the sun comes thru
on the window
after snow

BLUE SLEIGHS

December, the
water moves
dark between the
snow dunes in ten
thousand hills
pulling light
around the
black stones, a
sound to sleep
and love by
like bells
running thru the
children's sleep
when they dream
of blue sleighs

SEPTEMBER 26, 1996

this morning the pond
looks like marble. Rose
and charcoal dissolving
to dove, to guava, rouge.
Only mallards pushing
holes in the glass, so
unlike the pond, deep in
trees, almost camouflaged,
startling as coming upon
your reflection in a mirror,
just there under trees and
the wooden bar and the
driftwood benches blackly
jade with pines dripping
into it, shadows close to
my hair. What I didn't have
blinded me so I hardly saw
the small birds, blue,
pulling out of moss and
needles as if reaching into
the dark for their color

MID-NOVEMBER

when the black ducks come,
winter opens, a kick pleat in darkness

Eyelash fringe of ferns on shore.
Late fall thunder after a long
Indian summer.

Branches creak. Muskrat slither into
the pond like a stone the tide covers
in the glow of a stranger's flashlight

LATE NOVEMBER (1)

one minute, the sun was out, it was fall.
Geraniums under a quilt last night, a
        blotch of red opening.
On the front step what looked like lint
has small pink claws and feet.
Next the sky was the color of lead.

Geraniums under a quilt last night
like a child you've tucked in
or a body wrapped in the earth under leaves.
In the swirl of sudden snow, what
was left of the headless fur blows west

Like a child you've tucked in
whatever was living, a just-born
squirrel I suppose, hardly a living thing
        except for feet.
In fifteen minutes, the light came
back, cars stopped sliding

Whatever was living. Or just born
must have felt the wild snow was a warning.
I thought of the lover wrapped in dark
cloth and left in the leaves while, not knowing,
I took a ballet class. The geraniums

are still under a blue quilt this Tuesday.
One minute the sun was out, it was fall

GEESE AT MIDNIGHT

as if a feather
quilt exploded,
a white you can't
see in the dark
but breathe, a
wind of white
rose petals,
wave of fog
in the shape of
flying things.
Like radio
voices on
the pillow,
lulling, keeping
what's ragged
and tears at
bay, the geese
pull sky and stars
in through glass,
are like arms
coming back
as sound

LIKE A DARK LANTERN

I move thru the first
floor at 3 a.m., past
the cat who is curled
in a chair half made
of her fur, turning
her back on air
conditioning, startled
to find me prowling
in the dark as if I was
intruding on stars and
moon and the ripple
in water that spits
back the plum trees.
Grass smells grassier.
The clock inches slowly
toward the light. A
creak of wood and the
soft scratch on the blue
Persian rug the cat claws
gently merge with some
night bird I've never
seen like a poem that
goes along and suddenly,
at the end, like a banked
fire, explodes into the
wildest flame that finishes
off everything that has
come before it perfectly

IN THE RIPPLED EBONY COVE

Temperatures falling.
Moon slivers on the
rolling skin of water.
Geese in half light,
armada of feathers.
Wind blows them closer.
One silver band glows.
Their onyx, black flame
in a night fire

HORSES IN THE SNOW

if you are still, you
can hear ice crystals
move like beads
in blackness, before
you see them stand.
Under a snow maple
their legs lift in the
ballet step *pas de
cheval,* shake the
cold off, huddling
like children or the
memory of children,
shapes dark as
the space snow angels
leave, their hooves
an angel's tiara.
Light glosses the
gray as steam from
the horses rises

SLEEPING WITH HORSES

though I never have, I dream
of such warm flanks,
pulse of blood deep
enough to blur night
terror. I want my own
mare, sleek, night-
colored, to block
memories of the
orchard of bones,
the loved-lost under,
leaves, under a quilt
of guilt. I think of
cats, long slept with
then gone, how
the Egyptians buried
not only wives but
their favorite pets
near them to cushion
their trip to the
underworld. I want
this mare, velvety
as the dream mare's
nose, nuzzling my
skin in the black
that braids us into
one so I won't
move unless she does

THE YOUNG GIRL DREAMS OF ESCAPE

of a wild mane her
own hair tangles
with, her thighs
opening for the
horse's warmth.
She will elope
when the rest of
the house is sleeping,
carrots and apples
for her love.
She has cantered
through dreams of this,
the horse lover,
almost a part
of the harp of her
body. Night wind,
the mane a pillow
stars tongue.
This is not love
pressed up against
high school
lockers, a one-
night stand in the
back seat but
a whole world suspended

WHEN I THINK OF BARBARO'S BIRTH

of the foaling men
kneeling in golden
straw, his mare's
midsection heaving.
La Ville Rouge's
coat glistening with
sweat. I think of her
eyes rolling, her
groans and the men
each taking a foot,
the mare's nostrils
flaring. Night, a wind
of straw, manure,
sweat, dust, urine and
the night's cool air.
How they must have
wondered at the bay
colt's size as Barbaro's
wet and bloody head,
shoulders, torso and
black legs slid from
the mare. Down the
road, a truck backfires.
Flat on her side, La
Ville Rouge lifts her
head, looks at her new-
born colt sprawled on
the soaked straw,
eyes blinking, a scoop
of vanilla ice cream on
his forehead. I imagine
La Ville Rouge
struggling to her feet,
neighing softly to her

baby and licking him,
how Barbaro tries to
stand up, spills, his legs
rubbery, falling back into
the straw until suddenly
he stands, swaying like
a willow, takes a step,
jerky, hardly graceful
but the starting point

LATE NOVEMBER (2)

Today in Virginia, unseasonably cold,
      high only in the mid 30s.
I think of a night drive from Austerlitz
an hour north to bring in my plants, early September.
The sky tangerine, guava and teal.
My own house strangely quiet, my
cat at my mother's

When I think of a night I drove from Austerlitz
to bring in the plants, my mother young enough
to swoop up suitcases, my cat,
I was looking for someone. "Aren't you glad you
still have me?" my mother purred. The cat I
got after that one, now going on 21,
the ice yesterday a warning

I was looking for someone. Each time I
left my mother's rooms, drove thru
Vermont leaves there was an ache becoming myself.
When the wind tore thru yesterday, on the stairs, a
shape that looked like lint with claws.
Later I tucked the geraniums in quilts
like putting a child under flannel or leaves

That ache, a wind under my hair

My mother tucked in the earth.
The headless fur shape with its pink claws
or feet, on its back, a mystery.
Today in Virginia, unseasonably cold

HERON ON ICE

Pale salmon light,
9 degrees. Floor
tiles icy. Past
branches the
beaver's gnawed,

at the small hole
the heron waits,
deep in the water.
Sky goes apricot,
tangerine, rose.

Suddenly a dive,
then the heron
with sun squirming
in his mouth, a
carp that looks a

third as big as he
is gulped, then
swallowed, orange
glittering wildly
like a flag or the

wave of someone
drowning

FEEDING DUCKS, GRAY NOVEMBER

no swath of light,
no smell of warm
wood shavings. A
rain-coming scent.
Last leaf in wind.
Walnuts on the deck
bleeding ebony. I
think of houses of
ice where there is
no light, of men
carving snowbirds,
seals, caribou,
dream llamas as geese
fly up, a cloud of
feathers skidding to
the corn that floats
on the skin of water
the color of night

GEESE ON ICE

frozen, perched as
if listening for some
distant code,
news of a warm

front coming in
time. Meanwhile,
alerts go out on
local stations,

schools close
early. The "partly
sunny" never came.
30 percent chance

of snow. Trees tilt
east, the ground
hardens. Geese
take root as scarves

float in wind like
strange new flags

ON THE SHORTEST DAY OF THE YEAR

A woman went into darkness,
past the black ruby roses
and was never heard from again.
She moved quietly past
bleached grass a December day
it moved into sixties near Troy.
It was foggy and warm, very
much like today. It could have
been today. You probably think
this woman was me, it seems
there are reasons. But listen
I've never seen, only imagine
those tissue-thin roses and
that last minute before light
collapses. A garnet leaf
on the pond is less red than
my hair blazing, the lone
signal to guide you in

DOWNSTAIRS THE DARK STUDDED

with glow of
white branches,
clots of snow,
stars in clumps,
you have to bury
your face in
white. In
Syracuse, off
Comstock, the
lilacs just
starting, the
first man who
touched me
inside my
clothes pulled
me under such
white boughs
thru rain dripping.
Lacy boughs, light
filling the
dark orchard.
In this same
jeweled light
everything
opening like
these clenched buds

CHERRY BLOSSOMS IN DARKNESS

glow like
stars of lace,
heavy snow
clotting on boughs.
I couldn't sleep,
the sweet white
floating up
stairs pulled me
back to the
cove of an
old lover's
arms deep in
such white
dripping branches,
white petals
on slopes of
skin, lips
studding Tuesday
with jewels
in the sweet
grass, locked
like antlers

REPRIEVE

for the moment, my
cat, who turned her head
at chunks of just-
cut beef, now is nuzzling
nearly empty cat food
tins, purrs thru the
night. Limp as rags,
for a week under the
bed, she claws the
rug in the sun. I say
nothing, just listen
as I do to her crunching
food, lapping water
at 2 a.m. In stillness
the sound comforts
like bells or words in
Spanish or French
I don't understand. Her
chewing, like pearls
or amber warming to
skin soothes though it
is as untranslatable
to me as the nuances
under chatter in
the streets in Montreal
or Paris. Still, for
the moment, like music
or velvet, her paws on my
eyelids are a reprieve,
like June, or roses
or lilacs in early light
before anything scorches,
goes limp or loses
its rouge, while morning
glories are a necklace
of amethyst, exotic as
gracias, si, bon, merci

IT GOES ON

like dreaming of
some place after
you leave it. You
wake up in a daze

rain all day
in the pines.
It goes on
like that green,

like stained glass
between a bedroom
and the hall with
the light always

burning behind it,
cantaloupe and
peach light on
the bed all night

PLEASE NUZZLE SHEETS I'VE LEFT MY SCENT IN

(stories inside my head)

ROSE

when it's behind my knees
you'd have to fall to the
floor, lower your whole
body like horses in a field
to smell it. White Rose,
Bulgarian Rose. I think of
sheets I've left my scent in
as if to stake a claim for
someone who could never
care for anything alive.
This Bulgarian rose,
spicy, pungent, rose as my
16th birthday party dress,
rose lips, nipples. If you
won't fall to your knees, at
least, please, nuzzle like those
horses, these roses, somewhere

IF THOSE BLOSSOMS DON'T COME

if the tangerine doesn't
fill the house with thick
sweetness. If you put
your hands over your
ears one more time
when I'm talking. If
there's another month
of wanting to sleep all
day, the cat the warmest
sweet thing I can imagine.
If this damn rain doesn't
let up, I'm going to
have to rewrite the story
you've got in your head
about us and I don't
think you will like
the ending

WRITERS CONFERENCE BROCHURE

Sunny in the new flyer.
Everybody's smiling,
writing under the trees.
It doesn't rain, there are
no black flies. Flowers in
bloom. No one can see
the poet who will black-
ball you when you're
not interested in his bed.
Pine smell and night birds
camouflage the novelist
who packs in the night,
moans, "If I don't get out
of here I'll become an
alcoholic or gay." In the
photographs, the giddy
cradle their paper babies.
It's like a Christmas card
letter of the Happy Family
before what's really
going on leaks out

FASHION CITY

Have you ever dressed up in those
tawdry clothes? I'm asking because
tho I wear tight, low jeans, ultra-
sexy VS, find miniskirts superb
for running after a train, but I've
never been in one of those stores
with fur G-strings and lace panties
with the crotch cut out. How com-
fortable can they be? Or clean? I
know garter belts are supposed to
be sexy, especially with silk hose
and nothing else. Even a fake
cigarette in a black rhinestone
holder might add to the look. But
today I'm seeing the fishnet and
push-up black bra, the little apron
with nothing covering behind
not as vulgar but something else:
my friend's husband is not well.
She's crying, even at tap and ballet.
What you and even I might see
as sleazy, she is squeezing into,
pulling on with her fingers shaking
out of love. This isn't about yelping
Fuck you with the finger, but more
like a horse soothing somebody
scared, a mother cradling a feverish
infant. She is in what sounds to
me like something I'd have trouble
wriggling in or out of love,
she hooks and smoothes to make him,
after the diagnosis, forget what
could be ahead

WHEN I SEE SARAH JESSICA PARKER IS REPLACED BY JOSS STONE

for Gap, I'm thinking what
happens happened again:
the daughter replacing the
mother, blooming as the
mother starts to fade. I
rarely write about being
less young, a euphemistic
way to get around what
I'm thinking. It's like a
man clutching a tumor
growing big as a Siamese
twin. There and tell me
truly, can you stop looking
at it? In your mirror,
across the table. The lines
that never mattered
deepening, hair thinner.
When I saw Joss Stone
singing that Janice Joplin
blues, gorgeous taut
skin, Melissa Etheridge,
bald head, both belting
the blue blues out, Joss's
arms lovely, a white
I bet nothing has slid from
abruptly, leaving a burn,
a scar and sure she's
hot and her teeth are
lovely but I want Sarah,
I want her blues, her
over-30 beauty to
mirror mine

ISN'T IT ENOUGH HOW IT SLAMS BACK?

(what you can't erase)

DO I REALLY HAVE TO WRITE ABOUT WHAT SEEMS MOST SCARY?

Isn't it enough I've fought against
it with ballet classes every day,
often more than one? Do I have
to tell you about the letter
from a woman who says, "Now
in the gym the men stop looking"?
Do I have to joke, "Pull the plug if
I can't do ballet," laugh when a
friend says, "I didn't sleep with him
because I'd have to get undressed"?
Do I have to remember my mother
saying she'd rather be dead
than lose her teeth?
I think of the friend who
says she doesn't worry about what
poem she'll read but about what she
will wear. Another says she wants
plastic surgery but doesn't think
it's right for someone in the arts:
shouldn't she care about loftier things?
I think of another woman who will
be photographed only in certain
positions. Do I have to tell you what
I'm thinking about isn't death?

YOU CAN READ A LIFE STORY IN THE TATTOO

lives in a Russian Mafia film, each
symbol, a death, a slice of terror,
jail. The body's story, a short
story, a novel and if one lives
long enough, a trilogy, a serial,
something always with a surprise
ending. Today when I couldn't
wash off the Halloween tattoo,
soap and water soluble the
directions said but the snarling
tiger roared on. Only my pale
skin is a dark rose now as
if rage put its dark rose on me for
good. And I think of that
Japanese girl whose lover
covered her body with symbols,
not unlike what her father had
begun, each inked word or
shape a kiss, a brand. I expect
olive oil, some cream will
dissolve the fangs and claws
on my chest but what about the
tattooed man who undresses
for the first time, exposes
murders, assures his part in
torture to the woman without a
clue. And what of the woman
whose lover, addicted to
piercing her skin with his
needles, his brand, what about
her when all bare space runs out?

OLD BOYFRIENDS

The deaf ones leave a note in
the house you don't still wait
for him in, unable to call.
"For old times sake," he
writes. Or was it a blow job?
Others send postcards from
Miami, they've said the same
thing 16 years. Suddenly they
stop. Your present boyfriend's
daughter was 7 when the post-
cards came. Now she's wanting
a baby. Most, you never hear
from again. It's a jolt to read
their obituary, especially if you
left them. Almost a relief with
the ones you cared for too much.
No old boyfriends have called
me for dinner or brunch. Once
I could count them, the lovers,
at least waiting hours in an
airport with nothing to do.
They are probably on a list in
a poetry notebook in some
archives. I remember my cats,
from 6 years old more clearly.
Of course there weren't as
many. Old boyfriends come
back in dreams and when I
wake up I'm not sorry. One
writes poems about a woman
in clothes like mine who looks
like me. Hardly any have asked
for money or good wishes or
a marriage. The ones, never quite

lovers, haunt the most like a
book you couldn't put down
but never finished, left behind in
some abandoned railroad station
you won't get back to again

LETTER

the other day made it
hard not to think of
you reading in rooms
with strange light
and magical ceilings
so with water crashing

near the bed and a
green wind biting
the glass I wanted
to send you in the
damned poem. You
could press it
against a small cut,
it could make prisms

in your window spin
ivy into 12 slices
of the room. My
Swedish ivy is
dying, I forgot
what you said it
needed, but not
the rest

HOW IT SLAMS BACK, A LETTER USED AS A BOOKMARK

who could figure out
love? Not the old
blues men with
their whiskey and women,
women who've changed
the lock on the door.
Not Robert Johnson,
busted and poisoned.
Blues all around the bed,
the blues dogging,
dusting his broom.
How could some old
words make me remember?
Baby, won't you follow
me down. Old words.
No words. Even before I
started thinking of
him I knew if he
read this it was way
too late

REMEMBER WHEN YOU WONDERED WHAT "IT" WOULD BE LIKE?

From the first pages in *Love Without Fear*
where it said *if you let a man put his tongue
in your mouth you'll let him do anything?*
Remember when you thought you could
get pregnant dancing too close? How
fingers on the outside of a sheer white
blouse was one thing but moving in past
the bra strap felt like a bug invading. We
were shocked to hear Jessica's mother and
father took a bath together, naked. Somewhere
else, Heathcliff adored without touching.
Remember when some mothers forbid *The Snows
of Kilamanjaro?* Clitoris, a word I didn't
know but when I felt mine it seemed broken,
peculiar. And did you look forward to
blood in your crotch? Remember getting
the first Tampax in right, first diaphragm?
I was sure everyone could tell by the way I
was walking. And dear roommate, if
you are out there reading poetry, which I
don't suppose you do, remember how we
lay in the dark in the pea green room,
wondered what it would be like to have Dr.
Fox with his red beard go down on us.
Was it this, was it love that would rescue
us and keep us safe from getting into
trouble, which of course it didn't. Still,
somehow, older than parents with their
litany of "never let a boy," rarely, but once
on a velvet brown couch in the west with
the heat from his thigh a forest fire,
all I could imagine, all I wanted was to
know what he would be like

HAVEN'T YOU EVER WANTED TO USE THE WORD INDIGO?

the way it rolls off your tongue, blue,
mysterious. It's rather old-fashioned tho
but when you run out of words for the
blues, doesn't indigo give it a little
class? Then, I think of Millay with her
indigo buntings, curled on the same
velvet couches I have tho they've been
re-covered, not indigo but a chocolate
brown. One visitor stopping at Steepletop
in Edna's last years mentioned how
shabby the sofas were. I think how
Vincent gave up her velvets, lovers, drugs
for the stillness. Except for the buntings.
But I digress. Indigo. I had to listen to
The Indigo Girls, found I liked their name
better. I'd like to say I found the metaphor
to cinch this poem, to pull any reader
into Indigo ecstasy when I found some
e-mail about the film *Indigo Children*
but when I put the name on Google,
what I read lacked all iridescent blue,
that startling hypnotic glistening. Less
there than the marine's startling icy eyes,
indigo jolting as sequins from deep under-
ground as my real life pales

MONTMARTRE

Haven't you wanted, sometimes, to
walk into some painting, start a new
life? The quiet blues of Monet would
soothe but I don't know how long I'd
want to stay there. Today I'm in the
mood for something more lively,
say Lautrec's demimonde. I want
that glitter, heavy sequin nights.
You take the yellow sunshine.
I want the club scene that takes
you out all night. Come on,
wouldn't you, just for an evening or
two? Gaslights and absinthe, even
the queasy night after dawn. Wouldn't
you like to walk into Montmartre
where everything you did or
imagined doing was de rigueur,
pre-AIDS with the drinkers and
artists and whores? Don't be so PC,
so righteous you'd tell me you haven't
imagined this? Give me the Circus
Fernando, streets where getting stoned
was easy and dancing girls kick high.
It's just the other side of the canvas,
the thug life, a little lust. It was good
enough for van Gogh and Lautrec,
Picasso. Can't you hear Satie on the
piano? You won't be able to miss
Toulouse, bulbous lips, drool. Could
you turn down a night where glee
and strangeness is wide open? Think
of Bob Dylan leaving Hibbing. A little
decadence can't hurt. I want the swirl
of cloth under changing colored lights,
nothing square, nothing safe, want to
cancan thru Paris, parting animal
nights, knees you can't wait
to taste flashing

APRIL, PARIS

Nothing would be less shall we call it what it is, a cliché
than April in Paris. But this poem got started with some-
thing I don't think I could do but it reminded me of
Aprils and then three magazines came with Paris
on the cover. Sometimes I'm amazed at all the places
I'm not, let's say Paris since actually it's only March
but in the magazines they are at outdoor cafes which
must be quite chilly now. And I forgot the cigarette
smoke, until I see many in the photographs are holding
what I'm sure isn't a pen. I wondered how they can
always be eating, biting and licking something sweet
and still have the most gorgeous bodies. I wonder too
how my friend, once an actress, so maybe that's a
clue, could dress up in scanty, naughty, as she puts it
clothes for her husband while I am sitting here in
baggy jeans and torn sweatshirts. I'm wondering if it's
because he's lost his job and she is trying to cheer him up.
I began thinking of Paris when she described the umbrella
she decorated with drops of rain, how she just wore
a garter belt under it. I thought of tear-shaped drops of
rain I made for the Junior Prom's *April in Paris,*
long before I felt the wind thru my hair on Pont Neuf.
It's there in the photograph which I hope is more
original than the idea of the photograph because
I plan to use it on my next book. I wish I could feel
what she must, dolled up, trying to soothe this
man and getting off on it. As for me, only
imagining you, the one with fingers on me,
holding me on the page of a book
could make me as excited

THE WAY YOU KNOW

suddenly something is very
changed. It's like that
snow smell in the air.
You've noticed it,
haven't you? And know
the way it sends you
tumbling to decades ago?
Smell is the one sense
that can't be censored.
But sometimes just
a word in an e-mail, the
slightest dry brush
of lips lays the whole
scenario out. One shrug
of the shoulders of the
man my mother loved,
one *I may have a Yiddisher
name but that doesn't
mean I'm not goy*
and my mother knew,
as I do, tho we go on
living quietly

HAVEN'T YOU EVER LUSTED FOR THOSE RED SHOES?

(those aches in the arc of it)

BLUE AT THE TABLE IN THE HOT SUN

give him a shot of light,
give him ragged glass
to escape thru,
black cat blues dogging
the bed

He, OK, it's you, hell-bound,
in a hurry. You're pulling blue
out of the strings. Mama's got

a brand new. It's the table
in the light. Cat on the chair
with night scratching

Wind rattles the panes,
rattles gone love thru your
spine. Your baby's
changed the lock on the door

If you're still singing,
earth fills your lips

CHILD PRODIGY'S TIME TO DIE, SOMETHING GREAT MOM SAYS

Now, I have to ask you because I don't
get it. If you had a child that began reading
as a toddler, played piano at 3 and then
gave a high school commencement speech
at ten saying he was so different, so unusual
he "practically qualified" for the endangered
species list. Would you just smile, or think
something is weird? Imagine your child is a
child prodigy because he is, they say,
composing and recording music, winning
violin competitions, breezing thru college
with an IQ of 178. You've got, let's say, this
kid who masters everything. Photography.
Math. He just hurtles thru life like a meteor.
Then you come home and your little genius
is dead, there on the floor, a gunshot wound
to his head, a hole apparently he put there.
Wouldn't you be putting on your crying
shoes? Doing a wild "take a little piece of
my heart," Janis Joplin, wailing and moaning?
Wouldn't you shriek and wonder what you
didn't see coming? Would you just come
out and say, as if you were talking about the
weather, "earthly world didn't offer him
enough challenges and he felt it was time
to move on and do something great." Jesus,
if I were his mother I'd wonder, wouldn't
you, what kind of job I did homeschooling
him, wonder about him taking Independent
Study High School by mail. When she

says "he was so connected to the spiritual
world he felt he could hear people's needs and
desires and cries and we just felt like some-
thing touched him that day and he knew he'd
have to leave to save others." He isn't my
child, he isn't yours but I wonder if maybe
he saw some other kids he could have stayed

MAHO BAY, NEAR THE ASTROLOGER'S TABLE

yellow bird on
the table, two
curious lizards.
At the next
chair, Neptune
is rising, a fire
luring vibrations,
a time to invite
in. "You are over-
whelmed, even
cosmically," she
drifts off. I go
back to the piece
I'm working
on, the secret my
mother never
told me, as
mysterious

RING

Let's say you, even though you know I
mean I, found this ring in your mother's
closet in a shoe box of what mattered:
letters from the man she couldn't marry,
pale, blue ink on blue paper, bluesy
letters. Papers from the dog she would
never not long for. Then you see the ring,
Clara, etched on the 18K gold. Do you
feel you've been shaken by a ghost tho
the name's not familiar? Or maybe you
ask every living relative, most whom won't
be for long: *Who is Clara?* If I were you,
I'd write poems with that title, put the ring
in a safe-deposit box. What would you
think, before a trip to Peru, getting a
letter that Clara Lazarus died without a
will? Would you try to track her down,
you with the ring in your drawer or lock-
box? Go to the deaths in Wilmington
where all the Lazaruses lived? Let's say
you are leaving for Paris, not Peru and
the lawyers want you to sign. Wouldn't
you like some family history? Something
about this woman whose ring in a room
you used to sleep in mystifies? In testate.
They will tell you it takes so long,
how they will search Europe for more
relatives. Wouldn't you want to
know more about this Clara whose
finger is close to the size of your own?
The family tree they wrap the check in is a
mess. Jesus, you knew more not even
hearing of Clara. When you go to

305

slide on the ring, as if to enter her life the
only way you can, the ring is missing.
On the one you thought it was, nothing is
etched inside. After months of re-checking
jewel boxes, banks, would you begin
to think her name could have dissolved?
If it had slid thru your fingers, would
you think it is elusive as a soul?

HAVEN'T YOU EVER WANTED

The kind of lover you
will never get enough
of and if you did, you'd
have to die in his arms?
Haven't you wanted,
especially on a day like
today with buds on the
edge of unfolding, to
dance to death with a
passion you'd never
find in a normal lover's
arms? Don't you want
a dark fairy tale? Admit
it, not something out
of *Desperate Housewives*
but an all-consuming
love with the power to
destroy those who love
too much? I'm asking
you if you haven't wanted
to care so wildly, letting
anything come in the
way would be heresy,
get out your red shoes. If
you can't give me one good
reason not to give up
everything for passion,
let me try them on

FAT GIRLS

Once you've been one, you never aren't. "Chubette"
is a bullet that shatters a day of shopping. It is true,
isn't it, that once you've seen your self fat in 3-way
mirrors, or photographs, cringed when someone yells
"Fatso," you see that image at 120 pounds, at 90. I
stood on the edge of the scale so gingerly, I bruised
my instep. In ballet, if someone is losing weight, they
wear a yellow leotard or pale lavender but switch back
to black when they've gained a few pounds. "Zaftig"
only sounds nice but isn't. I will never believe anyone
truly loves dragging enough fat to make a separate
person around with them. Say "fat is beautiful," call
them plus sizes. Well though I know it's not PC, I
think it's a lie. Still, I think I shouldn't be writing this
poem, that it could annoy or hurt somebody, someone
who has tried to leave what they don't need to drag
around, what damages their heart. When you're
surrounded by ballet babies, spider legs and arms,
one anorexic, or bulimic, what isn't there seems to matter
more than what is. I think of my sister, once the skinny
beauty, who needed eggnogs to give her strength, until,
wounded maybe, she built a wall of flesh around her
you can't get through. Don't you think you've been
touched by all this? I think of the year I chewed gum to
not eat, got lots of cavities. Listen, I know this poem is
in trouble, in as much trouble as I will be if I finish it,
publish, or worse, read it. Once when I read a poem called
"Fat" at a woman's center, some walked out and the ones
who didn't were angry. But like the Shakers who wanted
everything stripped to the barest essentials, like an aunt
emptying her house of what she didn't need, I know there's

a lot I could get rid of. Here I'm talking about pounds but
if you took a look at my closets you'd see they are stuffed
with what I should shed: 5-inch heeled boots, Betsey Johnson
skirts, so much black velvet you could imagine yourself
under an enormous midnight sky, lost in the dark with
no light or exit

BAD DREAM #279, JUNE 22

I go back to Vermont, to Middlebury.
It's been a while, another lifetime?
And the uncles, the dead ones hover
in shadows, ghostly, their lips and
cheekbones on faces that some-
how aren't there but then, nothing is
as it was. The beautiful bookstore
with the flat above it where I dreamed
in my lavender back bedroom of
starring on Broadway or writing a book,
now looks like collapsing bricks about
to be bulldozed. This can't be. There's
no bookstore, no sign there's ever
been one. The bricks shift, the building
looks like something too dangerous
to enter after a hurricane, a house of
toothpicks one small breath could
make fall down. Even Main Street, a
perfect New England small town
where *Life* magazine came to photo-
graph this perfect calendar frame, the
red and green lights strung for Christmas,
children on sleds and of course the traffic
police who checked out every boy who
came to pick me up for a date my
mother would wait up for me from.
Have I been comatose a hundred years?
Where is the town I knew? What could
be left but mice and droppings in the
mostly abandoned street? Drug vials litter
the street instead of flower boxes and
geranium. When did the town become

a slum, a torn, blighted disaster? The
only color is grey. It's as if the mortar,
whatever held all that mattered together
dissolved. A heartbeat. Just the touch
of one brick and everything I thought I
could keep will crumble

ANOTHER BAD DREAM

the night was hard work, dreaming,
the strangers in the house
stain the air. I was going to be
abandoned. I could tell and finding
my crystal beads tossed on the
floor, apt to be cracked, turned to
rose dust didn't help. Or the man who
seems an intrusion stinking up the
bathroom. Before I slept, I was
appalled I had forgotten my Abyssinian
cat's birthday two days ago though
I remember it was the date Harper and
Row took my book. Was I the cat,
abandoned in my Sunday depression
though I always remember my cat before
her death Feb 11, 2002? The guests
seem oblivious to me, they are cocky,
the stingy, touching types. I wanted out,
to get out before I was abandoned.
Then I wake up shaking, horrified thinking
it's never been so long since I talked
with my mother. And then, like the
man with Alzheimer's, going thru his
daughter's death each time he sees
her in her coffin, remembering, awake
I can't go to see my mother,
she's dead

HOW CAN YOU EXPECT ME NOT TO WRITE ABOUT DEATH?

(waiting for something to bloom in this cold)

HOW CAN YOU EXPECT ME NOT TO WRITE ABOUT DEATH?

is there any other subject
splashed these last weeks
thickly across TV? Last
night I woke up wondering
how I could stand not
having my cat curl into my
skin, a fur doll, a breathing
pillow. How can I not think
of the bloated girl on the
feeding tube, legs splayed,
mouth connected to the world
by a tube for medicine and
food? Why wouldn't death
seep into every dream?
Who isn't thinking of their
wills, the funerals they will
or won't have? With the
Pope's body lying in state
how can I not think of my
mother's last hours, the purple
velvet they carried her
off in. It's April 4, I want
to think of the wild plum,
my favorite tree unfolding
slowly, like a difficult
birth

SULTRY, HUMID, RUNNING TO THE METRO

forgetting pills and running
back to the house, finally
on the train, a flash to that other
May, my hair just washed.
Chloe on my wrists and behind
my knees, your favorite blue lace
panties. Today time seems
botched. It couldn't have been
so many years since I slept against
your back, as many years ago
as your son was old, long enough
for me to have a daughter with
eyes as blue, to haunt me. The
green, maybe, a wall of it like
trees I drove through, that moist
avalanche of black emerald.
Or was it the tea rose leaking
on my skin made me think
of long, hot, hazy hours in your
kitchen, in different rooms,
moving toward your mouth. The
elastic is still good in those
lace panties, my hair is growing
longer, as if it was a flag
I could wave to let you know I'm
in town, as if you were living and
I was coming to you, still high
from a dance class where
when I stretched and warmed
up, it was as if for you

THE WOMAN ON THE METRO, ORANGE LINE, FOGGY BOTTOM

gray face, a collapsed wafer,
an apple left over winter on
some branch glazed in ice
that's melted. Not uninteresting,
like other wreckage, abandoned
houses that seem to have sighed
and then sunk into themselves.
Startling, raved, she takes out
powder first and dusts her whole
face, a silt of fine dust before
rouge, cheeks and chin as if to
pull your eye to what isn't pale
and lined. Then, lipstick. But just
as she is about to add what I
suspect will be a tawny shade,
burnt umber or rust, a man stands
in my view, it's as if someone
stood up, a giant, just at the end
of a movie. I wanted the last
face, the transformation, see
the stylish Washington women in their
black coats, perfect skin are now
here, faceless as some Picasso
or Modigliani face on their way to
see a lover, buy antiques. Trying to
look behind their mask, I miss
my stop

317

SOMEONE IS LOOKING FOR A WAY NOT TO DO IT

someone warns friends she is afraid
she will do it, slips out of jeans,
let's say, pulls on a sari. Each part
of her that didn't fit together will.
The weather is like her dress, hot
colors juxtaposed with fragile
pale shades, as she is. No one
will read her last note except
the one who can't share it. She
couldn't find a way not to, it
wasn't as if she hadn't told
friends, outlined her plans tho
no one expected she would bring
the baby with her. If a letter had
come at noon, if there had been
one person in the house with her
before she picked up the knife.
Her sari, the most flattering shade,
her lips the perfect rose color
she and her friends giggled over.
If the phone rang she couldn't
move to reach it. Was the baby
blue, cool? Did light fill the
borrowed house? What does it
mean when everything that hurt
her numbed her?

AFTER A DAY OF COLD RAIN

(it's more about beginnings)

MY CAT'S GOT SPRING IN HER BODY

cat poems, with their limited
audiences, the ones who cry
at the title of a book, order
17 copies. The ones who
groan. I mean, I've been
there, done the book. But
with this one, Jete Pentimento—
I called her that for her
leaps, horizontally. And
Pentimento, for my old cat
who died, Memento. I read an
art term that says pentimento is
a painting slashed over another
canvas, that eventually the
older shapes and colors come
thru. Not everyone cares
about animals I know
and especially poems that
smell of anthropomorphism.
It's more about beginnings,
moving away from what
decays to what is still full of
life, what could be like
the first time he slides down
your jeans and your thighs are
still marble. My old cat's death
was like my mother's: I put
the last photos of both where I
don't have to see them. Too
many people I know are
being stroked by death. That's
why I couldn't wait, brought
plum and cherry blossoms
to bloom in this cold

BETTER TO JUST LET IT GO

there's too little time, the cat
still leaping for flights. Alright,
let's not think of cats tho it can
be certain you can find one
if you had one. Or even let's
say your small dog, or retired
gray hound, there where you
take a photograph or take out
charcoals, knows this could be
the last time, could be a memento
(which was the name of my 22-
year-old cat I held in her last
hours, even photographed) but
you don't care about that and
she's in an envelope along with
my mother, skeletal after years
of wishing she could eat as
much chocolate as she wanted,
not get fat. What I mean is there
is too little time to hunt what's lost.
I saw it, the delicate script
with love, Clara and nobody
knew. No relative left knew who
Clara was. Better if I had dis-
covered her lonely in a home, or
in her own world. I would know.
"Who is Clara" over and over
on an 18K ring in my mother's
closet. Thick gold, what you'd
give a man. Not only who, but
why in my mother's closet?
"Love, Clara," in thin, etched

scroll, delicate as the ring wasn't:
Clara, Claire, a ghost. Never
real, no will, no daughter, no
cat. Clara, clear air. Not there,
unreal, ghostly, gone as now
even the ring is

MUSIC HALL

If there was a lover I could
imagine, his thighs would
take me over the brass. If
I could remember when the
bow or strings could have
been a tongue on the crevice
where a knee and hip join.
If I could touch what I feel in
the cat's fur or re-reading
Ruffian's last hours. I
think of the Cadbury in my
pocketbook, the winter once
he held me. In a drawer, the
violin's sales slip: 1921, sold to
my grandfather before
he changed his name, good
quality. German, 360 dollars,
so my mother could star.
It was the reason she named
me Rosalyn Diane, a name
for the stage. I try to remember
the feel of the strings. "Talented."
"Never screeched." I watch
the first violinist, rhinestones
in her hair, black velvet
skirt near the one with short,
stubby legs in what looks like
shorts she shouldn't be
wearing. The singer is nice,
making her cooing sounds. Years
after I throw glass as if to get
it out of me when my husband
ran off, he's at the box office
in line near me a friend says
and like this night, I don't
feel anything

COVE POINT

Some afternoons, in a certain
mood, there's a word, a name
I have to remember. Some-
times it's for no reason: the
twins I never could remember
until I thought of cameras in the
attic: Garret and Cameron.
Yesterday it was the ramshackle
casino, its name over the lake
where, for the first time, in
white shorts and tan legs, my
heart banged: would I be
asked to dance? And what of
"The Mocking Bird" with its
*kiss her in the center if you
dare?* You have to remember,
I was the plump girl with
glasses of course I didn't wear
those nights so a lot blurred.
I was the girl who won science
contests and art awards. To have
boys who didn't know I was
brainy, ask will I...was like
heroin. "Ramshackle Pavilion"
in a lost student's poem sent me
to Google, to Lake Dunmore,
Branbury Beach: nothing. I knew
it burned down as if it never had
been there. Chimney Point? No.
With so many of my friends
going, the name of this dance hall
where I first felt pretty is a comfort
I'm starved for. I e-mail VT tourist
sites, history sites with little

325

hope until in a warm tub I think:
diary, the little red one with a
lock that never worked there
near the bed. I turn to August
and there it was with seven
exclamation points and what I'd
been hunting for in so many
ways: Cove Point

HORSES

My sister was wild to work in the stables in Saratoga.
Cantering and walking in the cut hay on Flicka or Brandy,
clover
    in my hair, a comfort, always scary.
When my uncle took us to the harness track I brought a
book, hardly looked up.
My sister, insistent on having her way, and with a crush on
some jockey,
    planned nights in Atlantic City, mostly at the track

The clover wind soothed. Riding on back roads had nothing
to do with
    racehorses, strong and fragile as ballet dancers pounding
to the
    home stretch.
In Atlantic City in a green and turquoise sarong, my mother
kept her eye glued
    to the men glued to my 18-year-old body.
Wild to hold the hair of a horse like Charismatic or Ruffian,
I dreamt of merging with
    their hot speed as Daphne tried to merge with wood

Later, when we never visited enough my mother watched
the Derby and Preakness,
    longed to see another horse like Secretariat or Native
Dancer

I still long for men's eyes to ride me, be glued to my legs as
if I still was under 20.
Do horses know when they've won? Understand the crowds,
how they run for the roses?
These last years I don't want to leave the house for the jew-
els in the crown, have
    a terrible ache at such beauty and power it scares me,

like ice skaters
    one fall could destroy

Though my sister and I don't talk, we were both probably
glued to the screen this
    April Preakness. My mother would have been in heaven—
both of us on the blue
    couch watching and laughing, sure with the 3 of us so
close, no matter
    who won she was a winner

DOORMAT

I can still remember how
annoyed she got the first time
I used it, "Doormat,"
the way her mother let a brute
of a man walk all over her.
"Doormat"—you'd think I
called her mother whore or
bitch. Not strange, I went on,
so many women are at times.
I started a list of them: the
ones who faked orgasm to
keep some man, the ones who
say nothing when strangers
look and call their husbands,
"charming, so nice." Doormat
I say. I like the word. The ones
someone else wipes their feet,
their penis all over: what
woman, I want to say, without a
job, a good job and kids hasn't
had a stint keeping her mouth shut,
making excuses. One friend has
taken to buying cheap sexy
clothes, bustiers and fish-
net instead of painting. Door-
mat, dour mat. *Doormat*
I want to scream at my
aunt who coddles her 45-
year-old son who probably
steels her money. Even Hilary
was, I hiss, standing up for
him with his penis in who

329

knows whose mouth. I want
to say, maybe because I feel
so tired and hardly an Amazon
today, walking about, some-
one not me, afraid like all the
other DM's to say what I
am really thinking

IT WASN'T EVEN VALENTINO BUT TONY DEXTER, MADE UP WITH SLICK-BACKED HAIR, EYES OF SOOT

that stared thru me
at the Campus Theater
and made me always
choose men with dark,
foreign looks, men
from Iran or Greece
or Turkey. A glance
scorched, a tango and
I buckled. At 11, I
dreamed I was Pola
Negri, a name as
exotic as the words I
imagined whispered
deep in the tent of
his skin. I ached to be
his slave, his harem,
would grow clove
nipples, longer, lean
thighs. If he didn't talk,
no matter, I went for
quiet men, no blonds
I vowed, no Swedes.
Bad boys who would
not smile, strutting
boys, the hoods with
hooded eyes I'd write my
own subtitles for, my
hair, my words a veil I
could be what ever
I wanted to behind.
Blood lips, those

mahogany, tie-me-up
eyes behind dark glasses
let you imagine what
isn't as when Valentino
moved past the tent
flaps as if they were
labia

DON'T YOU MISS IT, THAT

smell of burning leaves? Color of fall, the rust smell, a smoky
amber? Don't you on some days want to splash, no, cover your
self in some scent that isn't light as lemons, doesn't smell like
something you eat like vanilla or blueberries. You can't imagine
the old movie stars not trailing a cloud of musk and heavy rose or
jasmine, freesia. They were there and they let you know. Some
thing from an animal's sexual gland. Something weighty and dark
and strong. Yves Saint Lent's Kouros and Rose Poiveres from a
rich cream from the anal glands of a civet cat, strong and clear,
persistent on skin. Structural, experts say, as an ocean liner, deep
as the ripe smell of a French trucker's jockey shorts after a muggy
day on A 51. One perfumer said her father loved the Civet cream,
the perfume made of butt cream and rolled it around in his mouth
and went home to kiss his wife. Sometimes the civet is cut, mixed
with banana peels, butter and children's excrement. Zubie cream,
"excrement d'enfants." Other scents made with horse manure plus
rubber, fragrances that smell of a trucker's unwashed armpit and
also like jasmine which smells like rotting corpses. Think of French
women still dipping their fingers in their vaginas and using a drop
of it on their wrists, behind an ear and it's not surprising some go
for what breathes life into their skin, like cream in soups or sauces,
why something hits you like a boxer's right hook and really would
you want to enter a room smelling of bananas or apples or bread?
Really, admit it, wouldn't you want to bring out the animal in the
ones you startle with something like Rose Poivree, even the name
unsettling, gorgeous and pungent with decay and mystery?

AFTER THE TOO-BLUE SKY DAY AND THE BLUE RISING

till even my fingers
go eggplant, how
could your e-mail,
dead 3 years, sting
full of the same fall
smells, your oaks
and maples burning
against rain. As if there
ever was any warmth
from you. Still, I can't
help looking back, it's
the way an accident
lures so you twist,
nearly crash. Or
how figures that
jumped from the
building in flame,
plunging like
broken birds,
riveting as words I
know end too but
still won't turn away
from his, "Hear the right
hand beg and beg,
taste the leaf
bark day," and then,
"maybe there's
some deserted island
in cyberspace
where we could
meet up, pull a few
corks, loll in the

surf and talk to the
sun. Surely some
tech geek has thought
that one up and be-
come zillionaire. Mean-
time: when/where,
indeed"

COMFORT AND LONGING

(and of course, more red shoes)

HERE IN VIRGINIA, THE MAGNOLIAS ARE ALREADY LOSING THEIR COLOR. OR, THE UN-AFFAIR

Even so, there was collateral damage.
Paris was a diversion, yes.
The last night in Austin we drove and talked
      till 3 a.m. in mist.
I would have named that night
      the last chance motel

Paris was a diversion, yes.
It wasn't the first time with someone who
      cared, mourning another.
Other bad news dogged me those weeks of rain

It wasn't the first time with someone who
      cared more for me while I longed
      for another.
Sunset from Pont Neuf would have made me
ache more if it hadn't been raining

Could it have been so long ago I was
      here with my husband?
It would not be the only time
      dying for one tortured man or another,
writers so tortured they could only torture

Longing seems so much more intense
      than skin on skin.
Wine helped and the beautiful Parisian girls
      with tight asses. Everyone was kissing in
the street. In Austin in thick heat the almost-a-lover
only grazed my lips with lips dry and cold

Wine helped. I thought with the margaritas I was
unfolding, wanted so wildly my fingers ached too but
I took my leather jacket from his hotel room
as if it was my body.

A year later, in the rain, what could have
felt as lost as the magnolias already losing their color

AREN'T THERE MORNINGS

after what seems like
17 days of rain,
and the one you're with
barking, a vicious dog
over nothing and you're
caught off guard, spew as
many sewer words as
he's slogged over you
but it's still dinner
and you have to sit, stony
across the small table.
Don't you want to just
pack a small suitcase,
get out, leave everything
behind? Of course
you can't, there's the
baby, the poems, the closet
of clothes you couldn't
ever replace. How could
you leave, your mother
still young, is smiling at
the railroad station about to
start out for an adventure.
When I think of my
mother, smiling with a
friend on a bench outside the
Middlebury rail station,
her black curls, teeth still
white and know how different
the years ahead will be I
don't even let myself
do more than barely notice
a man or two with dark

eyes on TV news, then go thru
the same routine where
I can try to hope the
night's dream will not be −
a nightmare

WHEN I SEE SHE IS READING THURSDAY

I think of the last
reading, halfway in
to chemo. I don't
remember her hair
any different but how,
after a few hours,
she nodded off. It
was the first time I
remember her with-
out a cigarette. Her
husband joking, she
applauded the others,
read a short poem
herself. Half a year
between when he
helped her out of
the chair, when they
left early and the
news: palliative
only, spread to the
pancreas, brain
stem. I sent yellow
tulips. "She will be
home in a few
days on e-mail from
her daughter. She's
had her favorite,
pepperoni. I'm not
sure she knows what her
friends know." I think
how she would
intimidate me with
her strength, took over
the room, the work-

shop, kept it in control
as I know she will,
reading as if there was
nothing special, one
more in a string of what,
like all she's taken
charge of, she is
sure she still can

EVERY DAY SOME PEOPLE ARE GOING HOME TO SEE WHO IS DYING

my graduate school office mate
with her father and grandfather
alone in a big Victorian said,
"I never know who'll be living,
who'll be dead when I come
home." For weeks, small girls
in pink pajamas are dying in
wrecked trailers under a heavy
pervert's garlic-stinking breath
or hog tied behind a rusty pickup.
Death shall have no dominion
Dylan Thomas said but lately it
is the main thing on TV. The line
between the living and dead
keeps moving. What does it mean
when you start to read the obits?
Every morning the ambulances
streak by the park I walk thru.
Someone tells me "lost at war"
is easier to live with than the
certainty of death. When Arthur
Miller died, who didn't think of
Marilyn going before him,
staying beautiful in our minds
as those who linger won't?

NOW LET'S SAY

you are out in the suburbs
in your little gated rooms
and you're not even
desperate. Let's say
you're not so young you
could leave whatever
seemed safe for a fling,
losing it all. Then the
red shoes mania gets to
you. Could be a love,
ballet, it could even be a
horse you fall wild for,
decide you want your
ashes scattered over her
grave. In your head maybe
you're Moira Shearer,
flame-red hair the
whitest skin, mystery skin.
Maybe the red shoes are
the color of what makes
you lie, something you
give up everything else for,
let what matters collide,
tear you to shreds. Are you
going to let this drug, this
hallucinogen slide through
your fingers, settle, be
earth or are you going to
put on those damn red shoes,
morph into a bird, some-
thing otherworldly as
the look in the dancer's
eye when asked, "Do you
want to live?" answered,
"I want to dance."

HAVEN'T YOU EVER TAKEN THAT ONE STEP?

you know, you put down
your leather jacket and you
know that means a whole
scenario past just staying
the night. It could start
with that first drink, first
kiss and instead of being
back where you were 24
hours earlier you're on a
train you can't come back
from. A touch, the last
margarita, a yes to "Would
you like to shower first?"
and the door shuts behind
you. It's not just buying a
pair of shoes you can't
afford like Ms. Bradshaw's
Manolo Blahnik high heels
but more like those red
shoes a dancer sees in the
window of a shoemaker,
blood red, glittering,
shoes her fiancé doesn't
want her to reach for but she
puts them on, begins to
dance, is high, her cheeks
red, her body glistening,
sweaty, soaring, leaping over
branches and leaves. She
is so tired but she can't
stop dancing as if the shoes
are part of her and she can't
stop dancing to death

MORE RED SHOES

Haven't you wanted to
put them on and have
everything that holds
onto you dissolve in
the rearview mirror?
Don't you want to be
flame? Be inflamed?
Haven't you wanted to
dance with a newspaper
that morphs into a man?
Maybe you wanted to
just get up from a pasta
dinner, walk backwards
to get a last look at the
room and plunge into
the weird reality of the
Red Shoes film? The
guavas and rouge tints
of Paris, Monte Carlo,
London mist and be
back in the forties when
everyone wore chic
clothes and were perfectly
mannered. But you knew
something smoldered
behind the veil of their
faces and you knew you
were stepping inside a
fairy tale where you won't
even think of that small
dining room you left with
canned peaches and a
clean napkin. You are
moth, Lorelei at once,

hypnotized, hypnotizing.
The eyes glued to you
once you slide into
those red shoes, (easy
as adultery) glue them-
selves to your blood,
become your blood as
you leap, smoke from
what is too hot to touch

WHEN JAMES DEAN SAID DIE YOUNG AND HAVE A BEAUTIFUL CORPSE

he was young and beautiful.
Sy DON'T YOU MISS IT, THAT lvia too, still with those
long legs even though she
might have had stretch marks.
Marilyn was in her prime,
Jim Morrison, pickled, had
to have been. Janis Joplin,
too young for crow's-feet,
lines. Sometimes it gets too
late to die young: write you
are a virgin and a suicide with
a body that has to be lovely,
but if you wait too long, it
is too long. Even JFK was
still a hunk. Think Valentino,
Harlow. But if you haven't
left by some age too sensitive
to mention, then it's too late.
Bardot, now, couldn't be
remembered pouting, that
gorgeous sex kitten. At a
certain point, people wonder
if you are still living. Soon
you'll be "Oh that guy, I
thought he was already gone"

DO YOU EVER WONDER ABOUT THE WOMAN IN ALFRED EISENTAEDT'S PHOTOGRAPH "VICTORY DAY, THE KISS"

the news of the war over.
Now 60 years later do you
wonder how she could have
bent backward, kept her
balance in those heels?
Let's say she is in her 80s
and still remembers that
rowdy day, the shots of
liquor and the good news,
how strangers (not worried
about herpes or Aids)
clutched and hugged,
smacked lips as if to hold
onto what was sunny
as the day. Did she go on
to have a life of children
with a man who puts up his
feet in dirty socks only
to find out the bloke was
cheating, remember those
arms? Maybe a face she
doesn't remember held her,
supported her as her own
man never did. And if years
after burying the one she
was relieved not to still
have in her bed, does she
still think of those strong
hands, recall the smell of
his wool navy, lips she raised
her hands to as if to say *take
me*. And are they more real
than anything else in her life?

DON'T YOU SOMETIMES, EVEN IF YOU'RE IN THAT

sort of love you don't
need to write about,
miss that first touch,
wildness? When you're
not sure you will but
you really do? When it
is still so new it's almost
electric and you don't
know his taste? Let's
pretend that first kiss
wasn't dry, a brush-
off even with the week-
end ahead and imagine
something that didn't,
is coming. Of course it
is a thick, heavy, southern
night and it's before
you realize his being late
to the reading wasn't an
accident, before he
won't show up the last
day when you'd have been
stranded except for a
woman you will leave
out: there's no reason for
her to be contaminated.
Forget the e-mail
before, seductive, more
seductive than any flesh
lover or the black hole
when you fly to opposite
coasts. Just think of the

moments you used to have
all the time with new men,
before one became what
of course you wanted, a
comfortable lover who
wouldn't leave you
vulnerable, knocking
skin off the knuckles in
your blood trying to get
thru. The light going down
behind palm trees you
want to forget rats live in
and he shows up after 3 years of
e mail foreplay with a screwdriver
since he doesn't know, forgot
to ask what kind of margarita
you prefer and you drink it from
the glass his lips have touched,
the closest you get to them and
there's a rush, your sheer black
tight dress sliding up and down
at the same time as you imagine
other moves in his arms and
those hunky legs, longer and
harder than you imagined

THE BELLY DANCING SKIRT

(costumes that merge with skin)

THE BELLY DANCING SKIRT (1)

When I put it on, it was
like putting on another body,
another life. "It's bursting
with my DNA," the belly
dancer smiled. I could
use a little of the Gypsy in
her, her giggle, soft curly
blond hair sun's bleached
yellow. I need that gauze
skirt with its coins jangling.
You'd know I was there if I
shimmied near your grave.
You could hear it long distance,
this me, wanting to be asked
to dance, my hips an SOS.
I want to jangle thru metros,
the new blooming cherries,
the mall like I'm the only
woman on the east coast
worth having. I'll shimmy
and twist so fast you'll never
see any flaws, cymbals in
my fingers hypnotic as
absinthe. I want you to
imagine more than you have
dared about me. I'll have
the right moves from the
dancer's scent melting with
my body, the skirt becoming
skin that no one, no lover,
no funeral director can ever
separate from me

THE BELLY DANCING SKIRT (2)

sheer lavender tossed
over a shape it
camouflaged like
words from you. It
rained all April.
On this first day of
pear and wild plum
exploding do I need
to have your screen
name tear open old
scars? Isn't it enough
to have you like a
pocket of cancer that
seals itself over,
there but no threat?
Something only the
autopsy of old poems
could find a link to?
What can I imagine
we'll do together
again that won't turn
another April leaden?
Tell me that you want
me to take off my
leather jacket smelling
of mold in a city I
haven't been in since
and carry me over in
the Motel Cheapo
threshold whistling
with that old grin?

THE BLACK SILK SKIRT FALLING

as if it was her,
something in her
leaving, stepping
out of her last
skin, chrysalis
about to be free
as the grackles
she watched those
last days. This
dream on the eve
of my mother's
birthday, there
was something in
the sound of her
skirt falling,
a pool blacker
than midnight
nothing was
reflected in. Then
the whoosh, the
wind of where
she was and then
wasn't. These days
of rain, as if to
wash her away.
Still, like the water-
fall outside our
apartment window,
she tumbles like
a river, so loud and
close to me I
forget she
isn't

SOME DAYS

Don't you want to just
be invisible? Go out
in one of those full-body
burkas? Of course even
then people would stare.
Haven't you ever wanted
to at least get rid of parts
of your body you can't
stand? Belly and chin,
maybe thighs and every-
thing that isn't as it could
be? I could tell something
was happening when I
stopped lusting for clothes
as if they were a man's
body, stopped dialing
VS late at night like
whispering to a taboo love.
In five-line diary entries
I often put down a favorite
or hated dress. Other
friends still bury depression
in shopping. Tho I did, it
no longer works, ineffective
as certain long-used drugs.
Look at me now, at the
kitchen table in faded yoga
pants and mismatched top
and my hair hardly flowing.
Don't you want to some-
times just *not* make nice or
look nice? Keep the phone
off the hook, stop checking
e-mail, not have to hear

about anybody else's prizes
or degrees, new books and
just decide to never again
go to any graduation,
any place you have to pretend
to be anything you're not?

IN SEEING A REVIEW WHERE MY EARLY POEMS WERE CALLED WILD

I think of the years in a
marriage, living like a
nun while readers
imagined me a flower
child, a hippy. Haven't
you found it odd how
someone pegs you by
how you dress? Some-
thing you wear on a T-
shirt, a flip phrase they
take as who you are?
And haven't you wanted
to fling back how you
were shaking inside
your cowboy boots and
a mini, going up to the
mic but few could tell?
Think of the dowdy
librarian (in glasses of
course, hair in a bun) in
too many movies who
becomes a sexpot once
her hair flows over the
backseat. No wonder we
have the saying, "Let
your hair down." When I
used "fuck" or "come"
in poems, I wasn't doing
either but some readers
would rather not know

SPIRITUAL

Have you noticed anything about
those who describe themselves
or their writing or painting as
spiritual? Do you cringe, as some
might at the words "fuck" or
"shit"? That, tho maybe crude,
don't offend me? The "spiritual"
aren't able to say them, out loud
at least. There's something about
the ones who say they are, like
others who say they're so glad they
live in the north or south or east
or west where people are lovelier,
imply of course that you probably
aren't. I notice those who keep
praising their spirituality say
you don't understand suggesting
it is because you aren't. But I
notice these "spiritual" people often
aren't. Isn't it phony to gush what
a godly person you are and then
dream a banishment room for your
husband, care more about money
you are making than about much
else? When the spiritual gush, does
your skin crawl too? Those
Pollyannas you could never be,
forget the mystical. And when they
end their e-mail with "Life is good
and it gets better every day if you
think it is," don't you just
want to go and take a bath?

IF I HAD A DAUGHTER

I'd be jealous of her
perfect skin, how she
would parade in spike
heels I have but no
longer wear. I'd long
for her slim body:
tho mine is, it's
not the same. At her
age, I was chunky,
in glasses, too shy. If
I had a girl of my own
I'd be jealous of her
pouty, dark, lipsticked
lips, a little Lolita
tho she wouldn't know
as she bloomed. I
know I'd feel my own
life shrink, my bright hair
dry out. Once I heard
you lose a tooth for each
baby. She'd be oblivious,
lost in the mirror never
imagining boys won't
want to dance with her.
Her smile would blind,
her eyes glow, enormous.
As she moves away
out the door, in them
I see my own reflection
grow smaller

HAVE YOU EVER GONE BACK

to where you were at 15, a
star at least in your daydreams?
You think about the people
you were with, the fat girl,
Judy Scott, who did things with
boys you never dreamed of.
Imagine them middle-aged in a
condo or worse. Today in the
science museum, I'm amazed
how young so many people
are which of course I was
with my exhibit on the eye.
Really, wouldn't you like to
be on display in a museum like
that? Be in a wilderness diorama
or have your own exhibit not so
different from a new prize-
winning book? Looking out,
I'm astonished how blue the
river is, the same one my mother
paddled down and then posed
with the man she couldn't
marry tho he signed the photo-
graph "to my angel." Don't you
wonder sometimes, not just at
science parks or metros, how
very, very young so many
are? I think of myself with
my science exhibit spread out,
an enormous papier-mâché
model eye half shouting
"Look at me." Sometimes I
can't believe I'm not still
that Rosalyn Diane, looking

ahead, as my mother must
have on the Charles, to some-
one small whose name she
would hang onto her wrists
and legs and when she could
no longer hold them, have
her go on to write that she had

WHEN DEATH COULD COME FAST ENOUGH TO LEAVE YOU AS THE NOT-THAT-YOUNG WOMAN IN THE COFFIN WITH CHIPPED PURPLE NAILS

Do you really want to
spend your time being
a good, being a lady?
Don't you want to put
a black line thru those
calendar dates for
things you said you'd
do but never wanted
to? Those graduations
and dinner parties
where you hear about
the African priest so
furious about condoms
he'd prefer AIDS, for
the 6th time? You don't
need to. Sip champagne
instead on the deck
and cut the phone cord,
put on beads or an
exotic, hardly available
man half your age.
Wouldn't you rather
paint in lace bikinis,
even the ones a dead
lover liked? You don't
have to pole dance in
Dupont Circle or
give up vitamins but
when the years dissolve
behind you like the

wake of a boat at
night or small towns
moving toward the Mid-
west, don't you want to
want what's wild and
light as glass in a
kaleidoscope, always
startling, gorgeous?

HAVE YOU EVER LOOKED AT AN OLD DIARY

and thought that was who I was
at 15 and I still am? Forget
an idea that when you're
older, what tore you up then
won't, that you're not ever to
reminisce about the boys
so electric you put only
initials in a diary with a 50-
cent lock, afraid the whole
name would scorch you?
Whoever said getting older
means anything but getting
older? Do you think I'll
toast wisdom or sense? Do
you really think there's
more and there's more that's
different? Look at your own
little apartment, your little,
little life and even if you've
won prizes—I've won some,
not the huge ones—but could
it be better, really different
than the few lines a diary the
old cover peals from, "went
to Morrisville and won 1st
prize" and all the exclamations.
Now, really is a yawn and is
ennui better than the litany
of boys who were dolls?
Or is it now you don't even
bother to look? And wouldn't
you like a day when the
big question is "I wonder if
I should pierce my ears?"

WHEN I THINK OF THE LIONS, THEIR CIRCLE AROUND THE MEWLING GIRL

how, kidnapped, held and beaten
7 days, she was crying, 12. She
was whimpering, mewling, the
sound maybe like a lion cub.
She was making that noise
when the lions rescued her,
chased off the abductors, the
men who had been beating her,
attacking her. Girls are raped to
give into marriage. The lions
heard something, scared them off.
Three lions guarded her, protected
her for half a day before police
and her family found them. It
could have been much worse,
young girls raped over and
over, deep in the black green.
7 days, beaten over and over.
Whimpering and crying.
This is why they didn't eat her

THE STARTLING, YOUR LONG E-MAIL

He read the spaces in
what I didn't want
to say as true, a
relief. Who is
seducing who in the
space where once
there was a rush
to leave? That you
said as much,
again. That I keep
asking questions
as if my words
still keep you
before I can delete
more than your name

HAVEN'T YOU EVER, LIKE I HAVE, WON-DERED, SEEING ALFRED EISENSTAEDT'S *KISS* OVER AND OVER

how that nurse feels
60 years later remembering
the news, August 14 light,
the shot glass filled over
and over on the street. Do
you think she compares
the smooth skin of her
arms to her 85- or 86-year-
old elbows and wrists, the
little you can see of her
as it would be from then on.
If she married, and she
probably did, did those
large hands, those strong
arms haunt her through
childbirth and Sundays when
nothing seemed as it should?
Did the remembered taste
of those lips help blur the
colorlessness?

I LIFT MY MOTHER TO THE COMMODE

almost too late tho
it's as close to the bed
as the tub to the
toilet lid I kept her
company on, handing
her soap and towels.
My mother, who could
climb Beacon Hill in
5-inch heels at 70,
can't lift herself with-
out my arms, my hands,
always too cold she
shivers. "If I just was
not so lazy," she sighs,
which translates, "Tired,
weak." The hospital bed
could be Everest. Our
awkward dance to lift
her hopeless as prayers
for mercy, a reprieve,
but I try to not show my
fear and now see her
tremble as the doorbell
rings. Verizon, to install
a private line she'll be
alive less than a week to
use. Still on the commode,
my stranded mother is
lifted by this smiling man
as if it was part of every
day's phone service,
gently as if carrying a
bride over the threshold
for a new life

THREE DAYS BEFORE MY MOTHER'S BIRTHDAY

I run into a young woman almost staggering across
the street. I'm surprised to see it's someone I
know. She seems pale. Then I see she's lugging a
cat carrier, and when I ask if the cat is OK, she says
no, a tumor. Seventeen years old. I think of my own cat,
just as old, how she has been drinking so much water,
and how this past year's been a gift, after the vet said
a year ago she was dying. A reprieve, an extra four
seasons. I think how, when she doesn't eat, I'm
afraid, how it reminds me of my mother's last
months. I shopped wildly for treats, something that
might tempt my mother as chocolate no longer could. I
bought her Popsicles in exotic flavors—blueberry,
mango, apricot—but still she kept shrinking until
we no longer weighed her. All winter, coaxed and
spoiled, my cat thrived, too heavy to jump up on
the bed. Now, with the air conditioning on, she chooses
a chair where it's warm and some days seems to be
slipping from me as my mother did, no longer worrying
about me when I drove home from the mountains
or caring what I ate or where. On her good
days my mother and I sat in the jade-light outdoors,
and I brought her watermelon, and strawberries and
cream, two of the few things she still longed for. Today
I opened extra cans of food for my cat, and she ate a bit,
but she feels lighter. When I brought my mother to my
house, I knew how her visit would end but not
how we'd get there, and I wanted to feel as if each day,
however it went, was a gift: I wanted to feel grateful, but
those last weeks she was like a kite whose string I'd lost
hold of, getting smaller and smaller

FORCED BUDS

They're blighted, but
beautiful still, like
what's forbidden,
scandal. I like them
best then. I know
that's the bad daughter
in me, not choosing
the ones that last.
I tore the branches,
sneaked them into
a blue jar the way I
might have had you in
the brown velvet couch
of a café I forget the
name of, let's call
it Casablanca. We'd
needed something light,
three hours of your
unhealing blues part-
way to making love. I
like the buds best
just on the verge of
opening, pink, pale rouge
as a nipple before every-
thing opens and falls
apart

FACING AWAY FROM WHERE I'M GOING ON THE METRO

The lost dead, some
still tugging from
underground with
their scotch on my
just-unwrapped
polka dot sheets.
The gone fingers,
each a book I can't
stop reading, photo-
graphs still in an
upstate bedroom.
I sketched the bed
they lifted my mother
from in purple
velvet, her shape
still in the egg crate
foam. Some days
I'm the snow lovers
made angels in.
And I'm also that
shape they left
night fills. Too often
it is best in memory:
mulled cider in barn-
wood rooms, mornings
under a mobile of
what was when
his cats were
my cats

THE GERANIUM

I am going to stop thinking
of the I'm-sure-dead geranium.
I know it's come back, like
a love you want to keep on
with since it seems there's
been so much you've been thru
together. The wild red flame
flowers, even before any
buildings burned, before any-
thing burned in me so wildly.
It's only a plant, not some-
one dying in a colorless
hospital room, their body
enough like a flower in water
that already smells. I kept
this flower going like an affair
I put too much in to leave.
And now I'm left with
what's dead

AFTER THE TSUNAMI

some are still crying,
some come to weep
but no tears come. Some
have lost everyone.
For some, this dooms-
day was more than their
minds could bear. In the
middle of rubble, a
young woman named
Nofal sits on the low wall
every day wrapped in a
blanket and sings. She
has gone mad. In her wild
eyes and laughter that
seems to come from some
deep, dreadful place she
sings everyone's song.
"All is destroyed. My
family, 8 or 9 people. All
gone, no more. I have no
phone. 45579, that's my
phone number."

DEAD GIRLS, DYING GIRLS

they are always the
smiling ones, the ones
you can't imagine
anything bad

could happen to.
Their white teeth
gleam, curls jaunty
as their grin, often

on the verge of a
giggle. They are the
girls you'd choose
if they were in a super-

market aisle, picked
to be hugged and
spoiled. Some are
kissing a dog, a doll,

a baby brother. You
want to kiss them,
want their photographs
to dissolve into flesh.

You want them to
walk back in thru their
parents' door though
they rarely do

THE DEAD GIRLS, THE DYING GIRLS

nobody can get enough of them.
In photographs, they were
beautiful. A camera

pans their bedrooms, the
sleeping pet that never barked,
small, pink sneakers in a corner

These about-to-be-dead girls
are carried like Scarlett O'Hara
in arms of a pervert

Nobody hears the door opening. Or
if they do, it's too dark for a face.
The girls are becoming famous

They will smile on in photographs,
pure and dead, on the piano,
beauties time can't touch

DEAD GIRLS, DYING GIRLS

no publicist could
get them as much.
They're on the air,
on Santa's lap,

in a costume with
a funny mask. The
girls are known
by their first names

like rock stars or
actresses. They
smile with a fake
nose at a birthday

party hugging a dog.
Their DNA stains
upholstery, is under
the last fingers that

tightened around them

WITH EVERYTHING OPENING, PEARS, MAGNOLIAS, CHERRY PETALS, APPLE, DOGWOOD

the dead bloom, planted so
long ago. You never expected
much from them. It's as if
with everything exploding, they
want you to marvel at them
too. The beauty of the plum
tree pales "short-lived compared
to us." "Yes, they are lovely,"
another sighs, "but remember how
I brushed your hair, washed it
in lemon juice. Doesn't that
count?" Sometimes the dead are
too loud, their fingers clutching,
hissing, "What do you remember
of the way I used to look?"
One newly dead reminds me of
the lilacs he left in a blue
Persian jar. The dead are sure
you would like to see them
and you would but you're not
sure how much to say, bring
the green emerald sweater you
bought too big for one to wear.
The new blossoms must want
to make the dead tell you what
they hadn't. They've been still
all winter, their season. I want
to just watch new life unfolding,
the mourning dove on her

nest, the wild plum, camellia.
But when I try to sleep with the
window open, the night bird
in blue wind, it's always my
mother's voice, "Honey, why
haven't you called?"

ON THE NIGHT THE MOST HANDSOME POET WALKED OUT OF THE SCHENECTADY COMMUNITY COLLEGE READING ALONE

headed up State Street
it was June, still light.
Alone. I couldn't
believe it. The last
raspberry light over
the old downtown
buildings. I watched
him pass Proctor's,
the only lit-up building,
past boarded-up cafés.
I could not believe
there was not a flotilla
of women behind him.
I had not written a
poem yet, I was afraid
to ask him to auto-
graph the book I
clutched. Alone. After
all the women he
left in tears. Sometimes
sent yellow roses to.
Sometimes mourned
on the page. Alone.
The most handsome.
Even years later
I could never tell him
it was like seeing
a Bugatti, a Lamborghini
somehow in the living
room to see him just
leaving alone,

strolling thru the town
empty as a de Chirico
painting while I stood
with my mother in
front of the bookstore
that no longer is,
held my breath

Acknowledgments

Poems in this book have previously appeared in the following journals:

5:00 AM, 13th Moon, Able Muse, ACM, American Poetry Review, Another Woman who Looks Like Me, Apple, Baltimore City Paper, The Baltimore Review, Before It's Light, Beloit Poetry Journal, Berkeley Poetry Review, Black Apples, Blue Line, Borderlands, Buffalo Spree, Caliban, Calyx, Canadian Women, Chelsea, Chicago Review, Christian Science Monitor, Clare, Coe Review, Cold Comfort, Cold Mountain Review, College English, Concho River Review, Confrontation, Connecticut Poetry Review, Connecticut Review, Denver Quarterly, Epoch, Event, Falcon, Fifth Wednesday, Fish Stories, Footwork, Frontiers, G.W.Review, Gargoyle, A Gathering of the Tribes, Gemini, Georgetown Review, Grain, Green Mountain Review, Greensboro Review, Hammer, Hampden-Sydney Poetry Review, Harpur Palate, Hawaii Review, Hiram Poetry Review, Hollins Critic, Icon, Israel Horizon, The Iowa Review, Jabberwock, Kaimana, Kansas Quarterly, The Ledge, Lilith, Lillabulero, Lips, The Literary Review, Long Shot, Lullwater Review, The MacGuffin, Main Street, ManGrove, Many Mountains Moving, Michigan Quarterly, Midwest Quarterly, Mudfish, New Delta Review, New Letters, New York Quarterly, North American Review, Not Made of Glass, OnTheBus, Painted Bride Quarterly, Paterson Poetry Review, Pearl, Pebble Lake Review, Phoebe, Ploughshares, Plume, Poetry Now Press, Puerto Del Sol, Rag Mag, Rain City, Rattle, River Sedge, Room of One's Own, Rosebud, Seneca Review, Slipstream, Sojourner, South, South Carolina Review, The Sun, Tangled Vines, Texas Poetry Review, Third Wednesday, Tikkun Review, University of Windsor Review, Untitled Country Review, Upstate Madonna, Verve, Whetstone, Whiskey Island, William and Mary Review, Witness, Wormwood Review, Writer's Forum, and *Yankee.*

I would also like to thank the publishers of the following books where these poems also appeared:

Persephone, Red Hen Press, 2008
Cold Comfort, Black Sparrow Press, 1997
Before It's Light, Black Sparrow Press, 1999
Another Woman Who Looks Like Me, Black Sparrow Press, 2006
All the Poets I've Touched, World Parade Books, 2011
Light at the End, Cleavis Hoof Press, 2009
The Licorice Daughter: My Year with Ruffian, Texas Review Press, 2006
Barbaro: Beyond Brokenness, Texas Review Press, 2009

Title Index

The New York Quarterly Foundation, Inc.

New York, New York

Poetry
Magazine

Since 1969

Edgy, fresh, groundbreaking, eclectic—voices from all walks of life.

Definitely NOT your mama's poetry magazine!

The *New York Quarterly* has been defining the term contemporary American poetry since its first craft interview with W. H. Auden.

Interviews • Essays • and of course, lots of poems.

www.nyquarterly.org

No contest! That's correct, NYQ Books are NO CONTEST to other small presses because we do not support ourselves through contests. Our books are carefully selected by invitation only, so you know that NYQ Books are produced with the same editorial integrity as the magazine that has brought you the most eclectic contemporary American poetry since 1969.

Books

nyqbooks.org

poetry at the edge™